CONTENTS

PHOTOGRAPHS (KEY):
(JW) John Winter, (SR) Mr Ranson,
(MP) Malcolm Parker
Cover Photograph John Winter

ISBN 0-86309-044-3

DISCOVERY GUIDES LTD © **1987**

MA... ....ounty
Du................ ed at
Gr........................Boys
between 1960 and 1967, before obtaining an
Honours Degree in Special Geography at the
University of London in 1970.

Utilizing his communicative skills, specialist
knowledge and understanding of landscapes,
he has become one of the country's most
published tourism authors. In addition, he has
been able to develop and utilize his talents and
interests in a range of other creative roles,
including consultant, script writer and
producer, for a wide variety of organisations
and media such as newspapers, radio,
television and video.

LORNE TALLENTIRE lives in Teesdale and
is a graduate of Oxford University. As a
historian working for the Christian Inheritance
Trust, Stockton-on-Tees, and having
investigated the medieval history of castles, in
particular Barnard Castle, and Teesdale, he is
now researching church and village history in
Cleveland. he undertakes Adult Education
Classes on Teesdales' local history in the
winter months.

WRITTEN BY MALCOLM PARKER AND
REVISED IN 1987 BY LORNE TALLENTIRE
MAPS BY PETER LEWIN
SERIES DESIGNER AND EDITOR:
MALCOLM PARKER
PRINTED IN ENGLAND BY GORDIAN PRINT
PUBLISHED BY DISCOVERY GUIDES LIMITED
1 MARKET PLACE, MIDDLETON-IN-
TEESDALE, COUNTY DURHAM, DL12 0QG.
TEL: (0833) 40638

Discovery Guides Limited wish to thank all those
persons, organisations, official bodies and their
officers, for their kind assistance in the production of
this publication.

Introduction to the Area

Teesdale enjoys the reputation of being the most complete dale in the whole of England. Within its borders can be found a large number of attractions, several being among the most important in the country. In fact, this single dale, where it has been said that 'Heaven meets Earth', is a major tourist area in its own right!

However, we must not forget that within this guide we are dealing, not only with Teesdale, but also with the surrounding area of the magnificent High Pennines which includes the tributary valleys of Lunedale, Baldersdale, Deepdale, Langleydale, that of the River Greta and those of a host of smaller, though substantial, becks and streams. The boundary of the area featured in this book also follows the Stainmore Pass enclosing Brough, the Upper Eden Valley and the Pennine's western scarp as far as the Hartside Pass, before enclosing Alston and the Upper South Tyne Valley. As a result there is a large and compact area to be explored and a great variety of 'treasures' awaiting your discovery...and at its heart, Teesdale, the greatest jewel of them all.

The highest point in the Pennines (and in England apart from the Lake District) is the summit of Cross Fell 893 metres (2930 ft) above sea-level. In fact it is on the eastern slopes of Cross Fell that we find both the stange and powerful Helm Wind and the source of the River Tees. It rises at a place known as Tees Head some 777 metres (2550 ft) above sea-level and from there makes its 75 mile (120 km) journey eastwards towards the North Sea.

Whilst on this journey it carves out a valley of great variety and interest. From Tees Head the river falls about 215 metres (700 ft) in the first 2 miles (3 km) cutting out a very rugged, narrow and steep-sided valley as it flows on over its boulder-strewn bed, rapids and waterfalls to High Force and the village of Middleton-in-Teesdale.

In this, the 'upper' stage of the river's course, we find that farming is generally limited to sheep rearing on the fells or moors, some beef rearing on the lower slopes and small dairy farms and hay meadows on the more fertile valley floors.

Downstream from Middleton-in-Teesdale the slope of the valley floor is much less steep and the valley gradually widens as we very soon meet that beautiful historic market town of Barnard Castle which stands as guardian to this part of the Tees Valley that we know as

Upper Teesdale. The river at Barnard Castle is very different from that trickling stream on the slopes of Cross Fell. By this time it has been joined by many tributaries including the river Lune and Balder and as a result is much wider and deeper.

The beauty and character of Teesdale is a direct result of the geology of the area. This is dominated by the shales, limestones and sandstones of the Carboniferous Period. These rocks have been modified, weathered and eroded in different ways and give rise to a variety of landforms. Added to these we have the Whin Sill to which we can attribute the presence of many impressive features. These include the waterfalls of Cauldron Snout, reputed to be England's longest and largest cascade, and High Force, reputed to be its largest waterfall. The River Tees itself along with its tributaries has played a dominant part in forming the present day landscape.However, it must be remembered that this area also suffered the effects of glaciation in the Ice-Age. In fact a glacier flowed down the Tees Valley and much of the straight-sided shape of the valley is a result of its passing.

Other characteristics of the landscape include the relics of the lead mining industry which according to local tradition has its roots way back in Roman times. Saxon and Scandinavian people settled here after the Romans, but it must be remembered that the first visitors arrived thousands of years before the Romans. All these people have left their mark, but the more visible historical remains are the much more recent Barnard Castle, Bowes Castle, Brough Castle, Raby Castle and Bowes Museum. Another aspect of history of which little present day evidence remains is that of the battles: the Romans fought the Brigantes near Stanwick St John about AD70; the Viking, Eric Bloodaxe, was killed in battle at Rey Cross on Stainmore in 954; King Malcolm of Scotland defeated the English near Hunderthwaite in 1070; Bowes Castle was attacked in 1173 by the Scots, and besieged by Henry Fitzhugh in 1322; Brough Castle was besieged and demolished by the Scots in 1174; Barnard Castle was besieged in 1216 by the enemies of King John, taken in 1265 by baronial rebels, fortified strongly against the Scots 1306-23, as were Brough and Bowes, and besieged and taken during the 'Rising of the North' in 1569.

As well as specific features to visit, there are also those traditional country shows and fairs which usually provide a good day's outing for all the family. Of these, perhaps the best and certainly the largest, is the Teesdale Country Fair. This is held every year on the last Sunday in April, but unlike the other major events in the area, this is only of recent origin. The first fair was held in 1975 and it has had a rapid growth. With displays, competitions, entertainment, local arts, crafts, and activities, and a large number of stalls selling a variety of products, its popularity is hardly surprising. Other events throughout the year include the Barnard Castle Meet which dates back some one hundred years. Held at the end of May, it is a popular traditional event though most of the traditional events in the dale are agricultural shows, such as the Bowes, Brough and Eggleston Shows held every September. Middleton has its own carnival, this year held at the end of July and beginning of August.

If you visit the Teesdale area then you will be in rather distinguished company of the past, including the artist Turner and writers Charles Dickens and Sir Walter Scott. Today it is also frequently visited by the Royal Family. Elizabeth Bowes Lyon, the Queen Mother, has been a frequent visitor as her family own land here, and Prince Charles, along with a number of politicians, comes for the shooting.

Other attractions include the large number of excellent walks, numerous sporting activities, a wealth of local stories and legends, and, of course, some of the most picturesque and quaint villages in all of England.

The "dawning of the dales" is the phrase used to describe the emergence of these Pennine hills and valleys from the approaching horizon. It has also been said that "all roads lead to Teesdale", and it is from the many panoramic viewpoints along these roads that its magnificent beauty can be enjoyed.

Teesdale, which, as stated earlier, still enjoys its past reputation of being the most northerly and most natural of the beautiful Yorkshire Dales, can be explored by following the country lanes into the quiet "backwaters" of the open moors, green valleys and picturesque reservoirs. Consequently it is not surprising that this area, often referred to as the High Pennines, was designated the 'North Pennines Growth Point for Tourism.' Therefore we can see that there is an enormous wealth of beauty, character and history stored in this part of the magnificent High Pennines. In fact it has benefitted from being a less well-known tourist area. But this will drastically change since the approval of the area as the latest official "Area of Outstanding Natural Beauty." Fortunately, to the relief of the many farmers who struggle to make their living from this often inhospitable landscape, there will be much care taken to protect and preserve Teesdale both for the people who live there and for visitors.

Furthermore, a new development to cover Environmentally Sensitive Areas (E.S.A.), has been established by the government in an attempt to 'turn back the clock' and adopt more traditional farming methods. This will help ensure the protection of wildlife habitats threatened by modern farming.

The traditional life of the dales seems to have changed little over the years and a very marked degree of independence and individuality is maintained. So whatever the reason for your visit to Teesdale and the North Pennines, please keep this area of outstanding natural beauty, unspoilt and beautiful, and the dalesfolk, many of them farmers, still friendly and helpful.

TOURIST INFORMATION

Further information about touring in the area can be obtained from the Tourist Information Centres listed below:

ALSTON Cumbria, The Railway Station
Tel: Alston (0498) 81696

APPLEBY Cumbria, The Moot Hall
Tel: Appleby (07683) 51177

BARNARD CASTLE Teesdale, 43 Galgate
Tel: Teesdale (0833) 38481

BROUGH Cumbria, The One Stop Shop
Tel: Brough (09304) 260

MIDDLETON-IN-TEESDALE Teesdale,
1, Market Place Tel: Teesdale (0833) 40638

USEFUL ADDRESSES

NORTHUMBRIA TOURIST BOARD
Aykley Heads, Durham City, Co. Durham, DHl 5UD
Tel: Durham (091)3846905

CUMBRIA TOURIST BOARD
Ashleigh, Holly Road, Windermere, Cumbria, LA23 2AQ.
Tel: Windermere (09662) 4444

COUNTRYSIDE COMMISSION
Warwick House, Grantham Road, Sandyford, Newcastle upon Tyne, NE2 1QF.
Tel:(091)2328252

Area of Outstanding Natural Beauty

Whether designated or not, Teesdale certainly is an area of outstanding natural beauty. With the beauty of its wild scenery, open moors, green dales, rare flowers, rugged rock formations, and its splendid waterfalls, it could not fail to be called anything else.

Since the C18th when men rejected formal gardens and turned to more robust landscapes subject to 'nature' and not 'reason', Teesdale has been famous. Garland in his "Tour of Teesdale" was one of the first to make it so, celebrating its towering cataracts, and even its nymphs who appeared at High Force. The romantic movement and the novels and poems of Sir Walter Scott, even though he did not celebrate Upper Teesdale, were to make wild scenery fashionable.

But it must not be forgotten that it is the inhabitants of the dale, in particular its farmers, who have tamed the sometimes cruel nature of the dale, especially in the winter, and here formed its hillsides at first in scattered strips or sections, and then in enclosed fields surrounding their small homesteads which made civilisation possible here. The inhabitants read far more than towns lower down the dale, there are fewer crimes committed, and although there are few wealthy inhabitants, most are independent and public spirited people who care for their neighbours.

A major debate has arisen in Teesdale over recent years, concerning whether parts or all of Teesdale should be included in an Area of Outstanding Natural Beauty designated for the North pennines by the Department of the Environment. Opposition has come from many farmers and estate managers that such a designation would mean further interference by other bodies in the normal working activities of the farmer, although the Countryside Commission has promised that this need not necessarily be so, if co-operation is achieved on all sides. In October 1985, a comprehensive enquiry was made into the matter, although it seemed wrong of those who opposed the scheme to claim that Teesdale was not an area of outstanding beauty. Eventually it was decided to designate certain areas of Teesdale, but not all, because of the opposition of the hill farmers to the scheme, but the matter is still being debated. It seems likely, pending the decision of the Secretary of State for the Environment in October, that the area west of Middleton will be designated, but not necessarily that east of Middleton.

Another scheme being considered is that of the government for encouraging farmers to use less fertilizer and to make hay later in the year so as to preserve the flora in the meadows, as well as the fauna. Entry into this scheme is voluntary but local farmers receive some monetary encouragement if they wish to join. Farmers further up the dale do not make hay until later anyway and this may encourage them to join the scheme.

Some farmers feel that they have looked after the dale all their working lives, and feel impatient at interference. It is probable, however, that these schemes will make very little difference to dale life, while preserving Teesdale's rare plant life, and encouraging the tourist trade in different ways.

The pretty Fairy Dell(SR)

It is true that tourists themselves can be a problem, and sometimes do not respect the environment. It is also true that although Teesdale is well known in Durham, its beauty is not widely known in many wider parts of England. It is likely, however, that numbers of tourists will increase, but not excessively, so that it is important that facilities and present and future tourist attractions are well advertised so that the dale itself can gain from the trade as well as the tourist! This guide will help in the fulfillment of that task.

Early Settlers to Middle Ages

To answer the question "Who are the people of Teesdale?" is not easy. This region of the British Isles has suffered the effects of numerous invasions of different peoples, each of whom have left their own particular mark on the landscape. In fact the nature of the landscape and way of life and character of Teesdale is a result of the countless generations of different people who ventured here and colonised the area.

The first visitors to the area, possibly some seven or eight thousand years ago, weren't colonists. They were probably Stone Age hunting parties who had ventured up from the coastal plains to hunt wild cattle. Avoiding heavily forested areas, they probably came from the west, and by high ground rather than along the river valleys. Their flint arrowheads and tools are the main evidence of their existence in the valley. They were helped by a better climate and cover provided by pine forest which about 5,000 years ago was replaced by dense oak and alder woodland.

The Neolithic (New Stone Age) farmers who gradually replaced them about 4,000 years ago were engaged in some cereal production, and cultivated small plots, cleared by their axes and burning. Examples of such axes have been found at Headlam, Forest, Bowlees and also Holwick.

The most remarkable survivals from the Bronze Age are burial and religious sites. These include the great burial mound at Kirkcarrion where an urn, now lost, was found in a burial chamber known as a cist in 1804; Bail Green in Mickleton where an encisted crouching skeleton was found; How Tallon on Barningham Moor where grave goods stretching from the Bronze Age to the Iron Age were discovered; and Egglesburn (Swinkley Knoll) where there is a burial chamber known as a 'round barrow'.

Burial places were opened up and used again, for to early man these sites demonstrated his hold on the land of his ancestors. Ritual sites include the Cup and Ring marked stones at Barningham, Gainford and Upper Teesdale, the religious purpose of which is unknown. The Standing Stones near Egglesburn were also for a religious purpose, but were broken up by 1809.

Iron Age sites in Upper Teesdale have been excavated by Dennis Coggins and Kenneth Fairless at Force Garth, where round houses were uncovered, originally surmounted by roofs of branches and centred on a farmyard. Arable farming and even metal working were

suggested here, and the valley was now being systematically cleared of trees. What connection, if any, such sites had with the huge Brigantian fort at Stanwick is unknown (this was probably the place where Venutius stood against the Romans).

The Romans, who were in Britain from 43 AD to 410 AD, saw to it that the northern tribe, the Brigantes, were kept in their place. They built forts in Teesdale at Piercebridge, Greta Bridge and Bowes, and their roads followed roughly the lines of the modern A66, A67, A688 and B6275. The road across the moor from Stanhope and Corbridge to Eggleston is also thought to be Roman, which makes questionable the idea that the Romans did not penetrate into Upper Teesdale. They may have come here to explore its mineral wealth as they did elsewhere. A Roman villa in Piercebridge, with hot and cold plunges and fine plaster walls, together with the palatial and extensive C4th fort there, suggest that Teesdale was not a "backwater" for the Romans!

The penetration of the boundaries of the Empire by barbarian invaders led to the withdrawal of the Romans to defend the Roman heartland. The British invited Saxons to help them stop invasion from the Scottish Picts, but these mercenaries revolted and then the battle was on for the control of Britain. In 598 AD, the Saxons overcame the Northern British at Catterick and the Northern English kingdoms were then established.

The Saxons settled extensively in the valleys and founded villages ending in -ton and -ham, both endings meaning 'farm' or 'settlement'. Many Teesdale villages have such endings but Cleatlam, originally 'Cletlinga', may be a particularly early site, and Eggleston may even indicate the site of a very early British Christian Church!

The centre of a dale in the Anglo-Saxon period was the village of Gainford which had a monastery by 801 AD and a church is mentioned by 840 AD when the whole area was owned by the monks of St Cuthbert of Lindisfarne who later settled at Durham. The villages of Teesdale were within a group known in this area as a "Shire". The Shire Court was probably held at Gainford and the church was probably a missionary church which served the whole of Teesdale. One of the boundaries of this estate was Dere Street, the Roman Road through Piercebridge, and on this road can still be seen Legs Cross, the remains of the Anglo-Saxon cross which may have acted as a boundary marker itself.

sent raiders! But it was not until 867 AD that they set up the Viking kingdom of York (Jorvik) which stretched to the Tees. The southern side of Teesdale was thus in this kingdom and the influence of the Vikings was soon felt in place names: thwaites - Crossthwaite, Hunderthwaite; bys - Naby; kirks - Romaldkirk; garths - Thringarth. The river Balder is named after a Viking god, whilst the word "Beck", so familiar in Teesdale, is also of Viking origin!

But what of the northern side of the dale and the upper Eden Valley. Norwegian Vikings who had settled in Ireland invaded Cumbria in the C10th, hence Kirkby Stephen (Church Settlement of Stephen). Ragnald, one of their leaders, after winning two battles at Corbridge, gave parts of Durham to his Viking followers Scula and Unlafball, but he gave the Gainford estate, which had been stolen from the monks, to a Saxon who had fought on his side. However, there are a number of Viking grave markers from Gainford which may or may not have been carved by Vikings. Saxon masons could have been copying the new style! It is thus unknown how many Vikings there actually were in Teesdale.

The Viking Kingdom of York collapsed when the last king, Eric Bloodaxe, was killed at Stainmore in 954 AD, but the Viking age had not finished. By the early C11th, the Vikings had won their way back, and a Danish King, Canute, ruled both England and Denmark. Canute had an estate which included Staindrop and Raby which he gave to the monks of St Cuthbert, now at Durham.

The last great invasion of the Islands occurred in 1066 when the Normans landed. Durham and North Yorkshire became a wasteland when the Normans harried the north, and King Malcolm of Scotland took advantage of the general confusion. He invaded Northern England and, while in Teesdale, won the battle of Hunderthwaite in 1070 AD. A large number of English noblemen were killed.

King William gave the southern side of Teesdale to the Earls of Britanny, who built Richmond Castle and who gave their Teesdale manors to underlords like the Fitzalans of Bedale who had a manor at Hunderthwaite, and the Fitzhughs who had Cotherstone, Mickleton and Lunedale. The Fitzhughs built their own smaller castles at Ravensworth and Cotherstone. The Earl of Britanny built another of his own to guard the Stainmore Pass at Bowes.

The next king, William Rufus, was not sure how much power to give to the church - in the form of the Bishop of Durham - or to the Earls of Northumbria - now also Normans. He gave the manors of Middleton and Gainford, and the forests of Marwood and Teesdale to Guy de Baliol, from Picardy, in 1093! Guy built his castle in old Marwood. His nephew, Bernard, converted it to a large structure of stone and founded a town, naming both "Bernard's Castle". The Baliols did castle guard duty for the king at Newcastle upon Tyne in return for their lands. The Fitzhughs and Fitzalans did two months castle guard at Richmond castle, for the Earl of Britanny.

Staindrop and Raby were still held by the monks of Durham, but a Norman Prior of Durham Abbey granted them in marriage to Dolfin, a descendant of the Earls of Northumbria. From this family they descended to the Nevilles. The Nevilles, on the other hand, were the servants of the Bishop and fought in his armies, hence Neville's Cross, the Neville Screen in the cathedral, and Bishop Robert Neville. The Manor at Raby existed in the C13th but a license to crenellate was given by Bishop Hatfield to John Neville in 1379 and most of the building of Raby Castle was originally of the C14th. The villages on the south side of Teesdale were all waste at the time of Domesday Book in 1086.

The Fitzhughs (although the family did not officially take this name until the C14th) in their charters to their subjects were very jealous of their hunting rights and often these charters appear to be eccentric and restrictive. However, they survived in Teesdale until the C16th so their fussiness must have done the trick! The Baliols often fell out with the Bishop of Durham, for they fought in the armies of the king - not the Bishop! They gave no land to the monks of Durham, but gave all their churches to a Yorkshire Abbey, St Mary's York, and established Granges and a horse stud in Upper Teesdale for Rievaulx Abbey and its monks, another Yorkshire foundation. John de Baliol was said to have been whipped at the door of the cathedral because he had fallen out with the Bishop, and promised to give money to found a college, later Balliol College, Oxford, but other accounts imply that this whipping was just a piece of gossip. The Baliols eventually lost their English lands when John's son, another John, became King of Scotland and fell out with the powerful King Edward I. During the later Middle Ages the Gainford estate was held by the absentee Earls of Warwick.

JERSEY FARM
Restaurant
&
Hotel

EVERYTHING YOU COULD WANT STRAIGHT FROM THE FARM

Resident Proprietors John and Jean Watson welcome their guests to the friendly family atmosphere of their home. One is free to look around the working farm, with its pedigree Jersey cattle and Suffolk sheep. There are many country attractions in the area, including the High Force Falls on the River Tees and the meeting of two rivers at Greta Bridge. Opportunities for golf, tennis, riding, pony-trekking, water-skiing and bowls are available.

A unique and memorable evening can be spent in our licensed restaurant within our farmhouse. We serve traditional English country fayre of the highest standard made from ingredients fresh from our home-grown produce.

OUR PEDIGREE JERSEY HERD SUPPLY ALL THE CREAM ON THE MENU.

Carvery open Tuesday to Saturday and for Sunday Lunch. Now open Sunday and Monday evening only for a new varied menu.

Whatever your choice, eat as much as you like in our popular FARMHOUSE CARVERY for your special evening. We cater for all entertainment.

● Dinner, bed and breakfast or bed and breakfast only ●

● Eight bedrooms looking out over quiet and beautiful Teesdale, all tastefully decorated with bath or shower en suite, colour TV and coffee making facilities ●

New for 1987, 6 luxury suites available with lounge/diner, kitchen, bathroom, double bedroom, hair dryer, trouser press, colour TV, in-house video.

A warm and friendly atmosphere awaits you by
JOHN, JEAN and MARK WATSON
'ENJOY YOUR STAY OR FARMHOUSE HOLIDAY'

WEST TOWN PASTURES FARM
Darlington Road, Barnard Castle,
County Durham DL12 8TA.
Telephone (0833) 38223
(One mile east of Barnard Castle –
easily accessible from the A1(M) via
the A67)

EGON RONAY
RECOMMENDED

The Bowes Museum

This magnificent dressed stone building always looks impressive whether viewed from near or afar. Seen at night from the high bleak, lonely moors on the distant southern rim of the Tees basin, its floodlit walls appear as a bright jewel in the darkness. Nearer, however, the view is even more impressive and from the gateway which marks the entrance to its 8 hectare park, the museum stands proud in all its grandeur. After all, this building which was designed in Second Empire style as a chateau or palace by Jules Pellechet is 92 metres long, 46 metres high, and cost John and Josephine Bowes some £138,000 during their lifetime and £143,000 as a legacy to the museum after their death.

John was born the son of the tenth Earl of Strathmore on June 18th 1811, and after a fine education and a period in public office, including a time as Member of Parliament, he took up residence in Paris. John was illegitimate and thus could never become Earl but he did have the Streatlam Estate worth £20,000. However, it was possibly his rejection which led him to spend so long in Paris. It was there that he met and became the patron of the actress, Denoite Josephine Coffin Chevallier. They had much in common, not least their love of art, and were eventually married in 1852.

Dividing their time between their home in Paris, their du Barry Chateau at Louveciennes and to a lesser extent the family home of Streatlam Castle in Teesdale, they continued to acquire more and more objet d'art. Eventually they decided to build a museum to house them all and after rejecting a possible site in Calais because of the unstable political situation in France, the present site in Barnard Castle was selected in 1864 following the sale of the du Barry Chateau in 1862.

The building work commenced in 1869 but the museum was not opened until 1892. A suite of rooms intended for Josephine were built on the upper most storey but she died in 1874. John, after a disastrous second marriage, died in 1885.

The objets d'art purchased included £8 for the famous El Greco 'The Tears of St Peter', 15 guineas for the Chile Pine or Monkey Puzzle which still stands in the grounds, and £200 for the Silver Swan.

Visitors interested in local history should go to the Regional Antiquities Section (formerly known as the Teesdale Rooms). Here can be seen Roman altars from Scargill Moor and Greta Bridge. The exhibits have recently been re-arranged and include a Saxon, Viking and Norman (Early Medieval) section.

On the first floor are rooms devoted to French decorative arts. See the Louis XIV guilt-bronze mask of a river god complete with fountain, the writing table used by Marie Antoinette, and the samplers made by children, mostly indicating the transience of life.

In the Gothic and Medieval Rooms are illuminated manuscripts, oak choir stalls, an altar piece made in Brussels, and a famous triptych. In the rooms devoted to British decorative arts, see the 1618 chimneypiece from Lanercost Priory, and the fine ceiling from Streatlam showing the ancestors of John Bowes, and their predecessors the Traine Family.

On the second floor are the famous French and Spanish ceramics and the picture galleries. Paintings include 'The Harnessing of the Horses of the Sun' (Giovanni Tiepolo), 'The Tears of St Peter' (El Greco) and 'The Rape of Helen' (Francesco Primaticcia). Here also are Canalettos, and works by Goya, Bourdin, Courbet and Monticelli. In other parts of the museum there are paintings by Gainsborough, Reynolds, Corot, Millet and Rousseau.

The Spanish Gallery has been rehung and a new catalogue will be coming out soon.

There are also the children's and the music rooms. Exhibits include Victorian stereo phonographs, a model of a fair, and a clock of 1780 with musical movements.

On the ground floor again the beginnings of the Museum can be noted in the Founders Room. Note the paintings of Josephine Bowes with their striking light effects and the model of the iron screw steamer, the original built to carry coal from the estates of John Bowes.

In the entrance hall is the famous Silver Swan - ask about times of performance.

This is only a fraction of the exhibits on display and make sure you ask for information about temporary exhibitions.

The grounds where picnics are possible, have been laid out with many decorative trees, lawns and flowers.

There is always something new to see and visitors will enjoy coming again and again.

Farming in the Dale

Whilst travelling throughout the dale one of the greatest pleasures is to survey and enjoy the natural beauty of the countryside. But how 'natural' is the landscape? After all, it is the product of man's influence over thousands of years, and ever since the arrival of the Neolithic settlers, some 4000 years ago, it has been subject to his farming activities. Yes, the landscape is far from 'natural' - look at the miles of dry-stone walls, the numerous enclosed meadows and pastures and the wide distribution of farmsteads. The dalesman is essentially a farmer, and agriculture the mainstay of life and prosperity in the dale - therefore no visit to Teesdale could be complete without some knowledge of farming.

Viewing the landscape with an inquisitive eye you will undoubtedly notice the large number of stone-built farms, and the fact that so many of them are white-washed, but how many of you will realise that it is the River Tees itself which marks the distinction. To the south of the river, much of the land belongs to the Estate of the Earl of Strathmore. Here the stone buildings remain 'natural' in appearance. To the north, however, most of the land belongs to the Raby Estate of Lord Barnard. It is the white-washed farms of this Raby Estate that provide a distinctive characteristic of the dale. It is said that one of the family of the then Duke of Cleveland had been lost in a storm and unable to find refuge. As a result the Duke ordered that all his farmsteads should be white-washed in order that they be clearly visible to the needy traveller. This tradition has been maintained to this day. Another characteristic of the Dale resulting from most of the land belonging to these two large estates is that the majority of the farms are operated by tenant farmers.

Although much of the land has been cleared in Teesdale since Iron Age times, and became more intensively farmed when the villages were first settled, the first real documentary evidence we have about the farms begins with the grant of lands in Teesdale to the monks of Rievaulx between the 1160s and 1180s by Bernard de Baliol, the younger. They were given common pasture on Monks Moor for a horse stud. They also had many sheep and cows. They had lodges at Friar House, Ettersgill and Hope House and a small chapel at Dirt Pit. Their work was done by lay brothers who were connected with the monastery but were not actually monks. Already, however, the forest on both sides of the river served as something else - a hunting ground. The Baliols, Fitz-Hughs and probably the Earls of

Warwick, all hunted in these hills and the expression 'Forest and Frith' comes from a deer park or "frith" that used to exist there. In the C12th wolves were also hunted in Teesdale.

On the other side of the river the Lords of Crossthwaite and the Fitz-Hughs agreed about 1200 that they would divide the profits of hunting equally between them.

From about 1230 a great hunting park came into existence in Marwood - and the chase is still remembered there in the 'Hagg' which means an enclosure. It was dispersed about 1630.

The early farmers in the dale in the C14th had shielings high up in the forest where they worked during the summer coming back down to Bowlees, Newbiggin and Middleton. But by the late C15th there were three important farms in Forest with various smaller farms under them, run by the Bainbridge family, and hunting was becoming less important.

Through most of the medieval period there were few compact farms; Stotley, Hudegill, Ravelin and Brockhalgill (Brochersgill) are some of those mentioned. The majority of inhabitants of Middleton and Newbiggin had scattered strips in the townfields. The agriculture of these fields had to be organised communally. Those possessing land in them had to make hay, harvest, or pasture their sheep and beasts at the same time or they paid swinging fines in the Manor Court.

Changes came by the C17th with a reduction in cereal production and a greater use of pastoral agriculture in the upper dale with the increased demand for livestock produce from the growing population of the Durham Coalfield. The grain fields became hay meadows which provided enough fodder to enable larger flocks and herds to be kept over the winter. In fact the size of flocks doubled throughout the C17th.

The next major change came between the mid-C18th and mid-C19th with a substantial increase in the number of farms in response to the growing population of the Dale, particularly as a result of the growing numbers of lead-miners who sought a small-holding of their own. Therefore a 'dual-economy' of mining and farming existed until the decline of mining at the end of the C19th. Today, many of the abandoned farmsteads to be seen throughout the Dale, especially on the higher marginal land, are testimony to the end of the lead mining era and the exodus of people from the area.

However, the C19th brought about much land improvement and in fact provided the foundation of our present farming environment. It was at this time that much draining of the land took place and that lime was applied to the land to combat the acidity produced by the leaching of the soil by the heavy rainfall. In fact, lime kilns were a common feature throughout Teesdale at this time. Sadly, few remain in good condition, but those found along Beck Road, Middleton-in-Teesdale, and known as 'Parker's Kilns', are perhaps the best preserved in the area. The first of the four existing kilns was operated by my great, great, great grandfather, Thomas Parker, about 1841.

Therefore, we can see how farming is a response not only to geology and climate, but also to man's activities over four milleniums. It is a hard environment in which to win an existence. The thin, poor soils and harsh winter climate preclude nearly all but sheep and cattle rearing. However farming is much easier today than in the past century when there was no electricity, no running water, no tractors or associated mechanized farm equipment. Those were the days of horse-power and the weekly trek to the market to sell the butter and cheese manufactured on the farms, as well as milk, eggs and livestock.

It is also important to note that local industries were those based upon farm produce, such as the production of leather and wool in mills beside the River Tees, particularly in the town of Barnard Castle. However it is the large expanses of wild moorland that dominate farming in Teesdale. This is the home of the hardy Swaledale sheep whose progeny are later fattened on the lowland farms. No other form of farming is profitable on these marginal areas. It is only the capability of the sheep to withstand the severe winter climate out-of-doors, including being buried for days in snow drifts, that makes hill farming a viable proposition. The foraging ability of this animal enables it to make the best of the short sparse grasses, albeit at densities as low as one sheep per hectare.

Beef cattle, even the red and white Herefords, let alone the hardy black, hairy Galloways can not survive at these exposed altitudes. However on the sheltered, milder, lower slopes and narrow valley bottoms they make a substantial contribution to the economy of the area by producing 'store' and 'suckler' calves for fattening on the lowland farms.

The farmer's year is certainly a busy one; the mating of the tups (rams) and the ewes in late Autumn, the supervision of the flocks throughout the long winters, lambing in April, shearing in early July and 'haytime' throughout July are of course essential events in the farmer's year. But let us not forget the Autumn sales of livestock at the local auction marts which are so much an essential ingredient of this rural area.

Farming is a continuing process with some change inevitable. Well, what of the future? The pattern seems to be one of amalgamation into larger, more economic units. This is a trend which has been noticed since the mid-C19th. For example in Harwood, Upper Teesdale: in 1850 there were 43 farms averaging 15 hectares: in 1973 15 farms averaging 67 hectares: and by 1993 there may be only 8 farms averaging 126 hectares. This will be achieved by an increase in mechanization and a decrease in workforce, but will result in further rural depopulation which in turn will bring about a reduction of services for those living in country areas. Nevertheless farming will continue to be the basis of the economy of Teesdale and as such should be treated with care and respect by the growing numbers of visitors.

Dipping time for the sheep(MP)

Lead Mining

The history of the Teesdale area is largely inseparable from the history of mining. Don't be misled into thinking that there are huge disfigurements to the landscape, you could not be further from the truth. The orefield here is simply an extension of that in the beautiful Yorkshire Dales, and the few remains that can still be seen, add an essential ingredient to the character of the area.

Tradition has it that the Romans mined the silver-bearing lead ores almost 2000 years ago, but to date there is no firm evidence to support this theory. But let us not forget that whilst it is lead mining that everyone remembers, this part of the Pennines has also been an important producer of iron ore, zinc, barytes, and to a much lesser extent, flurospar.

Iron mining was being carried out in the C13th in the upper dale, and by the next century they were already mining lead here. In 1421 the mines of the Earl of Warwick were under the guardianship of Robert Bainbridge (the first member of a family destined to become important locally) and were worth £6.13.4 (£6.66) which shows that they were already becoming important.

The minerals of this North Pennine Orefield are found in the Carboniferous rocks, though the veins in which they are found were intruded at a later period. The problem for the poor miner was not only that the veins comprised a variety of different minerals, but that they were also of indeterminate thickness and length. The assemblage of minerals in the veins are referred to as the gangue minerals, and of these, a metal content of 5% would be considered average, and one of 10%, a rich deposit.

To obtain the lead ore a variety of methods have been used down through history. The earliest mines were shallow pits along the backs of outcropping veins. Later mines in Teesdale built hushes in which the ore was hushed out by means of water held in an artificial dam. These hushes can still be seen in a number of places in Teesdale such as the V-shaped Coldberry Cut above Newbiggin. These were still being used in the C18th. Most of the early lead ore was used locally in the medieval period, for the roofing of Bernard's Castle for instance.

With the coming of the London Lead Company and other large companies, shaft mining associated with levels became common. These levels can still be seen in many parts of Teesdale, inclined to the foot of the shafts, the latter being used for ventilation in many cases.

In the C18th and C19th the work and life of the dale's leadminer was far from easy. He had to work very hard, with simple tools such as a pick, as well as in dangerous and unhealthy conditions, but such were the times that more miners came to the area to find work in the expanding industry. In fact, by the mid-C19th, about 90% of the working population of Middleton-in-Teesdale were associated with the mining industry. But many of the miners worked in remote mines and had to live in 'mine-shops' at the mines, only returning home every weekend or every other weekend. Times were hard; read about the early working-life of Reg Wearmouth!

Because of the low lead content in the ore, the ore was dressed at the mine. This involved the breaking of the ore into a size more suitable for smelting (often by hammer) and then it was washed and sorted at the 'washing rake'. In some cases, simple smelting was carried out at the mine site to reduce the bulk to be transported - a major consideration in the days of pack-ponies! But the vast majority of the ore was transported to larger smelting mills such as those that existed at Egglesburn, Langdon Beck, Newbiggin and Wemmergill.

Smelting had proved a problem in the C16th because of a shortage of timber. The result was that Flakebrigg mine was worth only £2 in 1560, and the mines of Upper Teesdale even by 1611 were valued at only £2. By the 1730s we find that many of the mines which were worked in the C19th were already in existence including Coldberry, Langdon, Shears, Willyhole, and Wiregill. The shortage of timber had been overcome by the use of coal.

The smelting mill at Eggleston was there as early as 1614, but in the C19th this was entirely rebuilt. This Blackton Mill lasted until 1904, although its chimney stood until recent times. The land for the mills here was leased to the London Lead Company by the Hutchinson Family just as the mines themselves were leased by the Duke of Cleveland. Both took royalties from the mines from the "Company"

With such mining activity throughout the area, one might easily gain the impression of prosperity, but for the miner this was just not so. One of the biggest problems was that the price of lead fluctuated greatly from month to month. As a result, the ore that a miner had won from the land, was often insufficient to repay the loan he had taken from the 'Company' to survive throughout each 'quarter' at the end of which he was paid. To supplement his income he had to make items to sell, and often had a small plot of land upon which he grew vegetables to help feed his family.

The largest single employer was the Quaker-owned London Lead-mining Company which came to Teesdale and established their headquarters for Northern England in Middleton-in-Teesdale in 1880. This company was quite concerned about the social and moral welfare of its employees. There was a free library in the Company Superintendent's house, Middleton House, built around 1830; the model housing estate of Masterman Place which was completed in 1824 to house company employees; the Assembly Hall, built in 1861 for the education of their employees' children and great encouragement towards the formation of a village band and other activities and events. However, their attitude towards religious instruction was remarkable. As well as helping to provide Chapels and Sunday Schools, they made it a pre-requisite for employment that each boy must have completed a satisfactory course of religious instruction.

Coldberry Mine Shop(MP)

With the bankruptcy of this Company due to the availability of cheaper, imported foreign ores, their mining activities ceased in 1905. This marked the beginning of an exodus from the dale in the search for work elsewhere, such as in the expanding coalfield of South-West Durham. However the legacy of fine buildings remains, as does the attractive Victorian drinking-fountain in the centre of Middleton. This fountain was presented to the township in 1877 by Robert Walton Bainbridge, having been purchased with the collection for his retirement as Company Superintendent in 1875.

An old mine entrance(MP)

As you drive around Teesdale, you will notice several reminders of these difficult bygone days. It is nostalgic to think about our heritage, and studies into mining activities are becoming more popular. If you wish to learn more about mining in Teesdale, then look out for 'Mining and Smelting in Teesdale' by Harold Beadle, the undisputed authority on this particular topic. But before you let your adventurous spirit lead you into an investigation of old workings, please remember that not only are these on private land, but long periods of decay have made them liable to collapse and therefore highly dangerous.

The Victorian fountain(JW)

Geology of the Area

If you look carefully at the rocks which make up the land mass of the British Isles, you may be surprised to find out that most of these were formed under the sea at a time when the climate was very different from that of today! You may have found shellfish in rock outcrops, stream beds, quarries or cliff faces - these are evidence that the rocks in which they are found are formed under the sea. In fact, since the earth was formed some 4,500 million years ago, its surface has been constantly changing. However, we can only work out geological conditions for the past 600 million years, and in this time we can see that the land/sea positions on the earth's surface have changed many times. The land masses have been broken down by weathering and eroded by rivers, ice, wind and sea, and the resulting eroded material desposited in layers on the sea-bed. These layers of sediment were then uplifted to form new land masses and mountain ranges. It is interesting to note that the rocks found near the summit of the world's highest mountain, Mt.Everest (8848m or nearly 9km high), were laid down under the sea and indeed contain fossils of sea creatures.

The geological history of the earth is divided into geological periods - just like a book is divided into chapters with each chapter telling its own story. The rocks which dominate the surface landscape of Teesdale belong to the Carboniferous Period which began 345 million years ago, lasted 65 million years, and ended 280 million years ago.

At the beginning of the Carboniferous Period most of 'England' was land, but the land was gradually sinking and a warm tropical sea advanced from the south and east. In the first half of the Carboniferous period (the Lower Carboniferous) conditions were characterised by the repetition of the sea becoming shallow and then deepening again very quickly. In the deeper sea limestone was deposited, but as the sea was infilled and became shallower, shale was deposited until the sea was shallower still, when sandstone was deposited. However, by this time the weight of sediments on the sea-bed was so great that it sank rapidly causing the sea to deepen and limestone to be deposited once again. This happened many times and each unit of limestone, shale and sandstone is known as a cyclothem. This rhythmic pattern of sedimentation, as represented on Widdybank Fell, is referred to as the Yoredale Series - so named because this successive sequence of limestone, shale and sandstone was first identified in the valley of the River Ure (Yore), known as Yoredale. Today this valley is better known as Wensleydale.

The first bed of Lower Carboniferous rocks, the Basal Quartz Conglomerate, was deposited unconformably upon older Lower Palaeozoic strata. These oldest rocks of Teesdale are the 500 million years old Silurian slates, which, though largely obscured by overlying rocks or surface deposits (such as alluvium or boulder clay), were once quarried for the purpose of producing slate pencils.

These slates were soft and greenish and were quarried at a small quarry near Cronkley and made into slate pencils nearby at a pencil mill. Their age has been shown also by the fact that grapholites are present in the slate.

The ruined stone building which was the mill was already deserted by 1890. Two millstones have been removed to Beamish Museum.

The thicknesses of the strata of the Lower Carboniferous are quite small with the one exception of a limestone band known as the Great Scar Limestone which can be found up to 30 metres thick.

Following the Lower Carboniferous Period came permanent shallow water conditions similar to those found in deltas such as those of the Nile and Mississippi today. Here great thicknesses of coarse sandstone were deposited. This is known as Millstone Grit and provides us with much of our typical Pennine moorland scenery.

As the deltas continued to silt up they became colonised by what became the great Carboniferous forests. These were similar to the enormous equatorial forests of the Congo and Amazon basins of today. It was from the compaction of this forest vegetation that the coal of the Upper Carboniferous Period was formed. However, it must be noted that rhythmic sedimentation associated with the deepening and shallowing of the seas also occured in the Upper Carboniferous. Shale, sandstone and coal were the rocks in this sequence. However, coal, which we use today in homes, industry and power stations, only represents 3% of the thickness of Upper Carboniferous rocks.

Towards the end of the Carboniferous Period uplift and folding of Carboniferous rocks began. This is known as the Armorican-Hercynian period of mountain building and it was accompanied by a period of igneous activity. An example of this can be seen in

the instrusion of the 60 metre thick dolerite sill (known as the Whin Sill) which extends over some 1500 square miles . In Upper Teesdale its black scars (in contrast to the grey limestone scars) can be seen in several localities such as the Falcon Clints, Cronkley Scar, and the waterfalls of Cauldron Snout and High Force.

An effect of the intrusion of the molten dolerite of the Whin Sill was the baking of the surrounding limestone rock, which now weathers on exposure into a soft 'sugar' limestone. It is on the soils developed from this limestone that many of the rare plants of Upper Teesdale are found today.

As a result of this igneous activity at this time, the mineralization of the Carboniferous rocks created the North Pennine Orefield. This has yielded over 3 million tonnes of lead ore and has been the most productive source of lead in the British Isles.

In the later stages of cooling of magna bodies, mineral solutions spread out through the country rock, following cracks, joints and lines of weakness. These are features common to the limestone of Upper Teesdale. On solidifying a variety of minerals was found in these mineral veins. The economic part of the vein was known as the ore and the worthless part was known as the gangue. Whilst lead was the major ore, gangue minerals included quartz, siderite, dolomite, fluorite, calcite, pyrites and barytes. Today some former gangue minerals are worth mining, such as fluorspar and barytes. In Upper Teesdale all lead mines have now closed but in the valley of the River Lune which meets the Tees near Middleton-in-Teesdale, can be found Close House Mine, the largest barytes mine in the British Isles. This dense, white, crystalline mineral, also known as heavy spar or barium sulphate, is used as drilling mud on the oil rigs, in the manufacture of paint and paper, and as a radioactive shield. Fluorspar, on the other hand, is an important ingredient in certain steel-making processes.

A more recent addition to the rocks of the area occured with the intrusion of the Cleveland Dyke in the Miocene Period, only 25 million years ago. This was at a time when much of the uplift and folding of the Alps was taking place.

The present day landscape of Teesdale is a result of weathering and erosion following its uplift from the sea. The two main agents of erosion that have been dominant here are the glaciers of the last ice-age and the rivers of the area.

The glaciers cut relatively deep and straight-sided, broadly U-shaped valleys, though these are not as pronounced as in classic upland glaciated areas such as the Lake District. Some experts believe that ice-sheet covered all of this part of the Pennines, but there is another 'school of thought' which suggests that some of these Pennine Hills projected through the ice as 'nunataks' (islands above the ice).

Following the end of the ice-age about 15,000 years ago the rivers of the area made their influence felt. They greatly modified the glaciated landscape and have super-imposed the characteristic features of normal river valleys though features of both influences can still be seen. Of the more distinctive of the river features are the waterfalls, whilst glacial features produced by erosion, such as the general valley shape, are much less significant. There are also those landforms produced by deposition, such as lateral moraines and glacial drumlins.

Therefore in simple terms we can see how the present-day landscape is a result of the actions of the rivers and glaciers upon the different rock types of the area.

Mighty Cauldron Snout(MP)

The Riches of Nature

This area is particularly rich in natural history, but anyone looking across the landscape must be aware that what he sees is not completely 'natural' but the result of the activities of man over the last 4,000 years. We shall look back at the changes later, but at first let us study the development of the area before the introduction of man.

You have already seen earlier in this guide how the area was glaciated in the last period of the Quaternary Ice-Age, which ended perhaps 12,000 years ago. The rivers of ice, known as glaciers, flowed down pre-existing river valleys scraping the landscape bare of soil and leaving large areas of exposed rock. When the glaciers eventually melted, as the climate warmed, the material picked up was redeposited along with the products of their erosion (the rock dust) in the form of boulder clay.

This boulder clay is impermeable and produces water-logged conditions. The vegetation which grew and died on this clay failed to decompose in the stagnant, water-logged acidic conditions because of the absence of bacterial and fungal activity so essential for its breakdown. As a result great thicknesses of peat accumulated, especially on the higher moorlands. The black and brown peat hags or peat brocks are very common throughout the area and are an important characteristic of the Pennine's moorland landscape. It is possible in some areas to see remains of birch trees indicating the presence of a former forest, partly cleared by man, but largely killed by a drastic change in the climate. It is interesting to note that our climate has changed drastically, even over the last 12,000 years, from very cold to warm and dry, to warm and wet, and finally to cold and wet. This has provided a changing natural vegetation in the area. In fact many of the rare plants of Teesdale are relics of a past climatic period.

The end of the glacial period meant an absence of soil and it has taken the thousands of years up to the present day for the present soils to have formed by the action of water, frost and animals breaking down the various types of 'bare' parent rock and mixing them with dead organic material. The type of soil depends to a large extent on the type of parent rock. Limestone rocks provide alkaline soils and sandstone rocks provide acidic soils. It also follows that different soils are the homes of different types of plants and grasses.

When the first settlers arrived in Teesdale some 4,000 years ago they were greeted by a far different sight from that we have today. The natural vegetation of the valley floors and lower slopes was made up of dense deciduous woodland of birch, elder, elm, hazel and oak. These people were the Neolithic farmers of the New Stone Age. However, they did not have tools to clear the dense forests so they settled and farmed the higher, less-wooded slopes and fells. With a growth in population and the coming of the Iron-Age, man began to clear the woodland from the valley floor to provide fuel, building material, living room and good farmland. This process has continued to present times forming the very different landscape of today.

However, we are fortunate that remains of the many habitats of the Teesdale area can still be found, although they are under increasing pressure from man, and there is always the danger that certain species of wild-life may become extinct. (It is interesting to note that among the list of extinct wild-life of the area are bears, boars, wolves, wild cats and wild cattle).

Throughout the countryside are many different habitats of varying size in which the plant-life (flora) and animal life (fauna) live in a delicate balance. The flora and fauna of each habitat depend on each other for survival and if one species of them is removed (by pesticide for example) then nature's balanced food-web is broken and the existence of the other wild-life is put in jeopardy. Here are just some of the habitats that may be found in Teesdale; woodland, haymeadows, hedgerows and roadside verges, peat moorland, grass moorland and the rivers. The wild-life found in each of these habitats varies greatly.

The woodlands offer the greatest abundance and variety of wild-life with each tree being a habitat in its own right. Different soil conditions influence the tree types which dominate, such as oaks and birches on acid soils, ash on alkaline soils, and alders and willows along water-logged river banks. It must be noted that some of the present trees are imports such as the deciduous sycamore and the various coniferous species.

Other changes take place with increasing altitude which makes the climate eventually too severe for tree growth. The absence of trees from the higher slopes and fells is evident throughout the dale.

Another difference is seen if the undergrowths of the floors of deciduous and coniferous woodlands are compared. The dense canopy

Come walking or touring in
East Cumbria
where wooded valleys, fellside villages and the high North Pennines can delight the visitor with superb landscape and fascinating history.

Walk leaflets are available to guide you on the best routes in the area, and a programme of guided walks is offered during the spring and summer. Alternatively, try a Fellrunner guided minibus tour as an introduction to the heritage of the area.

For details of East of Eden walk leaflets or the free Guided Walks and Fellrunner Minibus Tours programmes, contact

East Cumbria
Countryside Project
Unit 2c, The Old Mill
Warwick Bridge
Carlisle,
Cumbria CA4 8RR

· EAST · CUMBRIA · COUNTRYSIDE PROJECT

of the coniferous trees prevents light reaching the ground which as a result is relatively void of plant life, whereas in comparison the deciduous forest floor is light and boasts a wealth of flora which includes ferns, mosses, lichens and many flowering plants such as primroses, bluebells, wood anemone and honeysuckle. Birds are abundant too. They include the blackbird, chaffinch, robin, owl, woodpecker, songthrush and, along the riverbanks, the kingfisher and dipper. Animals also abound and include the small mammals; hedgehog, weasel, stoat, shrew, otter, grey and red squirrel, as well as the much larger roe deer. Insects are also worthy of mention and include the dragonfly and a variety of moths.

Another habitat, the hay meadow, is clearly visible to the visitor in June and July and it is very impressive because of its dense carpet of flowering plants. These include the dandelion, buttercup, kingcup, wood anemone, globe flower, orchids and meadow saxifrage. Animals include the hare, rabbit, vole, field mouse and there is sometimes evidence of the mole. Birds include the meadow pipit, skylark, redshank and lapwing. Insects are numerous and include wasps, bees and butterflies.

Other habitats include the hedgerow and roadside walls and verges which possess characteristics of the habitats already described.

The open fells contain several different habitats. The dry peat moorlands are dominated by ling or heather which provide a purple blanket over the Pennine Hills in Autumn. The wet peat moorlands are formed of and by sphagnum bog moss. These water-logged areas are also the home of white-headed cotton
-grass, the yellow-flowered bog-asphondel and the green-leaved sundew which catches and digests insects. Finally the grasslands of the fells, which divide up the brown-purple moorlands, offer another habitat in which we find a number of beautiful, though sometimes quite small flowering plants. These include the blue harebell and the yellow rockrose which are found among various grasses, sedges and mosses. Where springs appear we find wetter areas known as flushes which form their own habitats. In these wet conditions some of Teesdale's rare flowers are found. Flowering plants include the pink bird's eye primrose and the yellow mountain saxifrage. Several rare species are found in these fell areas based upon the soils derived from sugar-limestone. Perhaps the most famous of these is the Spring or blue gentian. Many of these plants

are protected in the Upper Teesdale National Nature Reserve. Another important reserve in Upper Teesdale is the remote Moor House National Nature Reserve located at the western end of Cow Green Reservoir.

The moorlands and the valley slopes possess quite a wide range of fauna. Birds include the golden plover, curlew, wheatear, ring ousel, ravens, black grouse, kestrels, short-eared owl and occasionally merlin and peregrine. Reptiles include the common lizard, slow worm, adder, grass snake, frogs and toads. Mammals include the fox, weasel, stoat, rabbit, hare, hedgehog, mice, shrew, mole, voles and occasionally the otter and the badger.

The water habitats of the ponds, rivers and reservoirs possess a different variety of wildlife. Many fish can be found such as minnows, sticklebacks, brown trout, rainbow trout and eels. Numerous insects, and reptiles such as the frog, toad and newt also thrive. Birds are numerous and you may see swallows, swifts and house martins competing for food during the summer, as well as a wide range of wildfowl. Regular residents have included the heron, mallard, teal, wigeon, goosander, kestrel, carrion crow, jackdaw, lapwing, snipe, redshank, blackheaded gull, dipper, curlew, wood pigeon, stock dove, dunnock, blackbird, mistle thrush, chaffinch, blue tit, great tit, long-tailed tit, redpoll, black grouse and reed bunting. Regular summer visitors have included the dunlin, short-eared owl, moorhen, redstart, spotted fly-catcher, songthrush, tree pipit, pied wagtail, yellow wagtail, wheatear and willow warbler. Regular winter visitors have included the whooper swan, goldeneye, common gull, greater black-backed gull, lesser black-backed gull, fieldfare, redwing, and brambling. Other birds which have made irregular visits to the area have included the kittiwake, rook, red grouse, coal tit, merlin, and black-throated diver.

The Teesdale area is very rich in wild-life though conservation of certain pressurised habitats is essential if we are to prevent the extinction of many species and preserve the quality of our countryside. You can play your part by NOT picking flowers (which would cause a loss of nature's seed supply), by educating others, by NOT damaging any form of wild-life (which could upset the balance of nature), and by following the Country Code.

To conclude I would suggest a visit to the Visitors' Centre at Bowlees. This is an informative centre for all age groups.

The National Nature Reserve

This huge reserve of some 3500 hectares (8600 acres) is of international importance and visited by scientists and botanists from all over the world. Therefore it may be surprising to discover that in its present form it has only been in existence since 1970 and that its initial designation was made only in 1963. However, we must remember that the conservation movement has only gained momentum over the last two or three decades, in response to man's more intensive use of the land and the increasing pressure placed upon many areas held in a precarious and delicate balance. The increased use of machinery, fertilizers, insecticides, as well as the draining and improvement of all categories of land, has led to the destruction of many habitats and the extinction of several forms of wildlife. In addition, there is the increasing pressure of competition for land from industrialists, house builders, and the need for more room for leisure and recreation activities.

The land protected within the Upper Teesdale National Nature Reserve has been subject to many of these problems, and it was to afford such protection that the reserve was established by the Nature Conservancy Council. Today the reserve covers a huge area from High Force to Cauldron Snout and incorporating Mickle Fell, Cronkley Fell and Widdybank Fell. The land to the south of the River Tees, owned by the Earl of Strathmore, was designated in 1963; that to the north of the river, owned by Lord Barnard, designated in 1969; whilst the final addition of land along the eastern margins of Cow Green Reservoir was obtained on lease from the Northumbria Water Authority in 1970.

Upper Teesdale has enjoyed a growing reputation for its unique assemblage of rare plants over a 200 year period from the end of the C18th, but it has only been in the last 20 years or so that very real fears developed about the irreparable damage and destruction of this very precious part of our nation's heritage. Prior to this time, remoteness, isolation and poor transport links restricted the attentions of too many visitors and hence the damage they could cause. However, in more recent times, improved communications, in conjunction with the advent of the 'family car' and an increase in leisure time, has led to a rapid growth in the number of tourists who come to the area to enjoy the magnificent beauties of geology and nature - and here in Upper Teesdale can be found several of England's finest landforms and some of her most impressive, unspoilt and beautiful scenery. Therefore it is ironic indeed that the majority of the problems facing the conservationist today result not from the desire of the visitors to see or pick the rare flowers, but rather, their wish to visit and marvel at the majesty and magnificence of the High Force and Cauldron Snout waterfalls, the dark, foreboding inland cliffs of Cronkley Scar and Falcon Clints, and the wild, bleak, unspoilt moorland fells which stretch up to the summit of Cross Fell, the highest Pennine peak. Another problem is that the popular, Pennine Way long-distance footpath passes through the heart of the reserve.

But what has made Upper Teesdale such a unique haven for so many species of plant and animal life? In simple terms it is the result of the interaction of geology and climate over thousands of years, but the full explanation is highly complicated.

The oldest rocks in the reserve are the 500 million years old Silurian slates, once quarried for manufacture into slate pencils. However it is the alternating strata of limestone, shale and sandstone belonging to the Carboniferous Period, which commenced about 350 million years ago, that dominates the area. Throughout Teesdale the frequently alternating outcrops of these very different rock types produce equally distinctive soil types and consequently an equally varied and alternating pattern of plant and animal life based upon them. But perhaps the single most important rock type found in the reserve is that known as Whin Sill; a dark, fine-grained, crystalline, igneous rock otherwise referred to as quartz dolerite. As magma, this intruded between the layers of Carboniferous rocks in the area during the earth movements of the later Carboniferous Period some 290 million years ago.

The extremely hard nature of this whinstone led to the formation of many of the major landforms of the area - but more important was the metamorphism of the surrounding sedimentary rocks by the intense heat of the igneous intrusion. Sandstones became quartzites, shales became slates but the Melmerby Scar Limestone band produced a crystalline, granular, sugar-like 'marble' known as 'Sugar Limestone'. The crumbly rock, sometimes referred to as 'calcite sand', is easily weathered, and being lime-rich and low in phosphorous is the most important single reason for the continued existence of some of Teesdale's rarest plants. In fact, the importance of Teesdale in this context is clearly illustrated when one considers that it

is on Widdybank and Cronkley Fells that can be found the only extensive outcrops of sugar limestone in the British Isles.

It is also important to remember that as well as the outcrops of solid geology providing different parent rocks for the development of soil and associated vegetation, there is also the surface geology to consider, in this case glacial clays which overlie much of the area.

Climate, as well as geology, has played a major role in determining the plant life of Upper Teesdale. One clue is the realization that many of the rare species of flora are arctic or alpine - in fact relics of the Ice Age which commenced some one million years ago. Since the end of the Ice Age some 15,000 years ago, these plants have gradually colonised the area with different species favouring the different soil types and conditions prevailing upon them. Since that time it is a result of the altitude (over 500 metres above sea-level) and the associated harsh climate that competition from more prolific species has not materialised. Another reason for the continuance of this delicate 'foothold' is the grazing of sheep - one might ask how 'natural' the plant-life is when it is a result of man's organised farming activities that the coarser grasses are eaten and the specialist plants allowed to remain!

Within this enormous reserve there is a rich variety of flora and fauna including the peculiar shapes of the extensive thickets of Juniper found on the south bank of the River Tees near to High Force, as well as the birch woodland found both above the Force, and below it, in Keedholm Gorge. This woodland is typical of the natural vegetation at one time common in the dale. Surprisingly, we know a great deal about the past climates and vegetation of the area because an accurate record has been safely stored in the peat deposits! The waterlogged nature of peat prevents decomposition of vegetable matter. As a result, remains of past plants (and animals), seeds and pollen grains, possibly dating back some 10,000 years, are preserved and can provide an historic record by examining a section through the peat.

In the Late Glacial Period about 10,000 years ago, after the glaciers had melted, the climate was very cold and only the hardy vegetation could gain a foothold, largely in the form of low density pine and birch woodland along with some willow, juniper, grasses and sedges. As the climate became warmer (in fact much warmer than today) we entered the dry, Boreal

Period where the juniper and willow disappeared, birch declined, and new colonists were hazel, elm and oak woodlands. The climate continued to change and about 7,000 years ago, the warm, wet Atlantic Period began, marking the decline of the pine and the advancement of oak and alder woodland.

The next significant change came about 5,000 years ago at the beginning of the Sub-Boreal Period when the climate became much less warm and drier. In response, the vegetation adapted with the rapid development of heathers, sedges and grasses which led to extensive peat formation. The climate continued to cool and about 2,500 years ago came the Sub-Atlantic Period which was cool and wet, causing heathers, sedges and grasses to continue to thrive with the hardy birch alongside the hazel, oak and alder woodland, as well as some ash and pine.

Therefore we can clearly see how vegetation has altered in response to climate. But let us now have a brief look at the plants of the reserve themselves, for many of these are relics of glacial and late glacial periods whilst others are remnants of the warmer, more-recent climatic times; a 'rare' mixture indeed, with species represented from Arctic to Mediterranean climates.

To enable visitors to enjoy these marvellous plants, the Nature Conservancy has developed the Widdybank Fell Nature Trail. This is a 2 mile return trip from the Weelhead Sike Car Park (and toilets) overlooking Cow Green Reservoir, to the thunderous roar of the Cauldron Snout waterfall. However it is a walk undertaken mainly by people wishing to enjoy the peace and beauty of the area or to experience the magnificence of England's most impressive rapids. Nevertheless it provides an excellent opportunity for those with an interest in wildlife to examine the rare species and the influence of alternating rock types upon them. The trail (which has free admission) follows a narrow tarmac road alongside Cow Green Reservoir and as such, there should be no need to get your feet wet or muddy unless you decide to descend to the foot of Cauldron Snout. Along the route there are some 14 major places to stop and study. These are clearly outlined in the official trail guide which should be available from the dispenser in the car park.

Where impervious clay overlies the soil geology, peat has developed and, upon it, heather and cotton-grass. In contrast, the

THE SHEEPSKIN WAREHOUSE

Come and see
our vast range of quality products

Choose from our wide selection of sheepskin coats
and leather garments

also

LEATHER HANDBAGS, SHEEPSKIN MITTS, HATS,
GLOVES, RUGS, etc.

Also we have an impressive selection of knitwear, made from the
pure wool of Herdwick, Swaledale and Icelandic sheep.

**AS YOU CAN SEE WE CARRY A WIDE SELECTION
OF NATURAL PRODUCTS, COMPETITIVELY PRICED.**

**We suggest that you compare our prices and quality with
others – we feel sure you will be impressed.**

Please come and see for yourselves.   Shops at:-

5, Newman Way	23, Newgate Street	37, Market Place
Battle Hill	MORPETH	BARNARD CASTLE
HEXHAM	Northumberland	Co Durham
Northumberland	NE61 1AN	DL12 8NE
NE46 1BB	(0670) 57860	Shop: (0833) 38149
(0434) 605594		

The foaming waters of Cauldron Snout(MP)

green limestone grassland is the home of a greater variety of flora, some extremely rare. On the better-drained limestone soils can be found, among the blue moor-grass and sheep's fescue, whitlow-grass, spring sandwort, heath dog voilet, wild thyme, common rock rose, fairy flax and the harebell. However it is mainly upon the extremely lime-rich sugar limestone that can be found the rare Spring gentian, Autumn gentian, Alpine bistort, sea plantain, and false sedge. Another interesting habitat is the water-logged, lime-rich areas, often near springs and known as 'flushes', which provide the home for yellow sedge, carnation sedge, the rare false sedge and flowering plants such as bird's eye primrose, Scottish asphodel, butterwort (carniverous) and yellow mountain saxifrage. Of course these are only a selection of the species to be found, but never-the-less should be sufficient to whet the appetite of the ardent botanist. (Please remember that these plants flower at different times of the year).

'Conservation' could be accused of creating many of its own problems because to enclose an area as being of special importance and to develop, as in this case, a nature trail, undoubtedly attracts tourists when the attraction of tourists is emphatically discouraged. Since the designation of the reserve the construction of Cow Green Dam and Reservoir and the development of the nature trail, annual visitors to Cow Green have been estimated in excess of 70,000. A low figure indeed when one considers the beauty and wealth of interest to be appreciated.

However, though severe problems are created by visitors not following the country code, the biggest danger to the plant communities of Widdybank Fell came from the construction of the 550 metres long Cow Green Dam which commenced in 1967 and was completed in 1970 at a cost of £2.4 million. There had been an increasing demand for water from the growing urban population of Teesside, but perhaps the greatest thirst was that of the expanding industry of ICI at the mouth of the river, so far away that it takes 2 days for the water to travel the distance. In the 1950s it had been using 18 million litres of water per day but by 1980 this had risen to over 250 million litres per day. As a result a dam and reservoir had to be built in the Tees Basin and although several locations were suggested, the Cow Green site was deemed to be the best. Here there was an ideal catchment area, firm foundations for the dam and the minimum of good farmland to be lost. However the conservationists put up a strong fight before losing. Sadly 10% of the most important grassland was flooded and some of the most important communities lost, despite an intensive rescue operation of transplantation.

Today, however, the existence of the 2 mile long reservoir still creates problems for the reserve because it is now, in its own right, a natural attraction; thousands of visitors often picnic in the car park overlooking the waters which are backed on the horizon by the lofty peak of Cross Fell, at 893 metres, the highest Pennine summit. But by far more serious is the immediate problem of the wind causing waves to undercut the shoreline of Widdybank Fell at the rate of 1.5 metres per year! The problems of the conservationist are endless!

To conclude, it must be said that no visit to Upper Teesdale would be complete without having experienced the wildness and grandeur of this very unique part of England.

Barnard Castle

Barnard Castle is a fine market town situated on the north bank of the River Tees and facing the highland reaches of Upper Teesdale. It is an excellent centre from which to explore Teesdale and the High Pennines, being only about 10 miles(16km) from Middleton in Teesdale, 18 miles(29km) from Brough, and 34 miles(54km) from Alston.

The town itself is extremely picturesque and interesting. There are not only many riverside walks where features of great beauty can be seen, but also amongst the present buildings of the old town (which dates from the 1130s) there are some of considerable historic importance. Before Barnard Castle (both castle and town) was founded by the Baliol family, there already existed a settlement in Marwood, whose ancient common pastures and open field systems were taken over by the new town hence the old rhyme "Marwood was a town when Barney Castle was none, and Barney Castle was built wi' Marwood stone". Today part of Barnard Castle is still in the civil parish of Marwood. Guy de Baliol first acquired the north side of Teesdale in 1093 from King William Rufus, the Conqueror's son. His family came from Bailleul en Vimeu in Picardy and Baliol is the Latinised form of this place-name. He probably built the first castle before 1100. This was sited next to the Old Roman Road from Bowes to Binchester as it forded the River Tees. The good defensive and strategic position of the castle on the Scar Top rock outcrop, which rises over 20 metres almost vertically from the river's edge, was improved by Guy's nephew, Bernard, in the C12th. He rebuilt the castle in stone, and the town which gradually grew up around it took the name of Bernard's Castle.

The first castle built by Guy was probably of wood with some stone features, as at Richmond. The massive curtain walls which still exist today were built by Bernard who extended the castle to four wards, and built its complex system of moats and ramparts. The building was continued by his son, another Bernard. With the outer ward, the area covered was extensive which enabled the people of the new town to bring themselves, their families and their cattle into the enclosure in time of danger or invasion. The Round Tower or 'dongon' as it was known in the Middle Ages, was built somewhat later (perhaps 1200), but its fine spiral stone vaulting, arrow slits, spiral staircases within its walls, and its garde-robe chambers (toilets), make it the most imposing and interesting part of the castle. Its preservation ,when much of the castle was raided for building stone, is

partially due to its use in the early C19th as a shot tower for casting shot, and as the home of a hermit!

Hugh de Baliol, a friend of King John, defended the castle against his baronial enemies, and a shot from a crossbow killed one of the leaders of the rebels, Eustace de Vesci, Lord of Alnwick, when he had raised his helmet while looking for a weak spot in the castle's defences; this led to the siege being raised.

Barnard Castle's last and most famous siege came in 1569 when Sir George Bowes, a staunch Protestant, defended it for the Crown, who then held the Barnard Castle and Gainford Lordship against the Earls of Northumberland and Westmorland, who wished to restore the old religion of the Roman Church and to free Mary, Queen of Scots. The siege lasted 11 days, probably from the 3rd to the 13th day of December, 1569, in the cold of winter. The numerous rebels brought large cannons to besiege the 800 men inside but it was not until the 8th December that the walls were breached. Even then it appears the rebels got in because those guarding the outer gates had gone over to the enemy. The other wards were still held but the defenders had little water because those who had defected had fouled the town ward well with two dead horses. In desperation those inside tried to escape by scaling the walls, 35 breaking their necks on the rocks below. The siege had ended in victory for the rebels, but 400 of the men left inside were allowed to ride out with Sir George to meet Queen Elizabeth's reinforcements coming north. The siege had been won but the rebellion lost. Sir George carried out executions by martial law that winter in the snowdrifts; 120 from Barnard Castle were executed, perhaps on the old gallows in Galgate disused since the time of Henry VIII.

The Baliols made Barnard Castle into a borough although it never, until recently, had a mayor. The people of the town, known as the burgesses, had houses for their trades made up of long thin plots known as burgage plots. These burgage plots can still be seen on the north side of Market place and the south end of Galgate. The other side of Market Place was not developed as early because it would have obscured the line of fire from the castle. There were thus no burgage plots on this side and, in fact, the present day gardens of the shops here are in the outer moat of the castle, and there are garden sheds against the castle walls! If you enter any of the lanes on the Bank which lead to the Demesnes you will also see evidence of the burgage plots where 'undersettlers' had their workshops and homes on the land of the more important "burgesses".

Newgate was probably the next street to be added. A hospital providing for the old and infirm was built there in the 1230s by John de Baliol. Then came Thorngate and Bridgegate. Bridgegate occurs in a document of 1391 and a bridge is mentioned in 1327. There were also smaller streets off the main streets known as 'wynds'. The Castle Wynd went from the Market Place, where the King's Head now stands, to the main entrance of the castle. Later the south side of Market Place was built, some of it from stonework taken from the castle. The Golden Lion is dated 1679. Gradually the growing industrialism of the town led to a concentration in the Thorngate/Bridgegate area with narrow streets, and monotonous yards which were to be so fatal in the cholera epidemic of 1847. The richer inhabitants moved out to the north to Bede Road, and beyond. Today, much residential development is in this area and in Startforth, the old houses in the Bridgegate area having been demolished.

Blagraves House, on the Bank, is mainly C17th but has a medieval cellar. It was probably an inn in the early days and has connections with Richard III, and John Forest, the Keeper of the Wardrobe at Barnard Castle for Richard III when he owned the estate. A secret passage is said to run from here to the castle. Cromwell may have dined there, but all we know for certain is that he visited and had a meal within the town in 1648.

The Market Place and Horse Market is full of fine old Georgian buildings and old inns. Note especially the Raby Hotel, Midland Bank and, of an earlier date, the Golden Lion; on Galgate, the Commercial and Three Horse Shoes are also Georgian; on the Bank, the Old Well; and Dickens stayed at the King's Head in 1838 while researching 'Nicholas Nickleby'.

The first church in Barnard Castle was probably the castle chapel, but a new church was built at its present site before 1200. A great deal of the interior is transitional and Early English, but the tower was built about 1873-4 by C.H.Fowler. Note also an effigy of Robert de Mortham, who founded a chantry there, who is said to have been a monk at Egglestone Abbey and also vicar of Gainford! The Perpendicular Chancel Arch is said to have the carved heads of Edward IV and Richard III. The first Methodist chapel, Broadgates, can be seen on the Demesnes.

Mention must also be made of the famous Market Cross, built in 1747 as the old Town Hall, which is often referred to as the Buttermarket. In 1804, two local men stepped out of a nearby inn to settle a dispute as to who was the best shot. Taking aim at the weather vane on top of the Cross, they fired in turn. Today, the two bullet holes can still be seen in their target. A short walk from the Market Cross is found the internationally famous C19th Bowes Museum, which is named after John Bowes, the 10th Earl of Strathmore, and his French wife Josephine. Not far from the museum can be seen the impressive ruins of Egglestone Abbey, founded about 1190 and in use until the 'Dissolution of the Monasteries' in 1540.

At the bottom of The Bank, below the Market Cross, is the ancient County Bridge, which, lying below the high castle walls, formerly marked the boundary between the counties of Yorkshire and Durham. As it was repaired in 1569 following the 11-day siege of the castle in the 'Rising of the North', the first bridge must date from before this time. A bridge there is mentioned in 1327 and 1422 although this is not necessarily the present bridge. But it is likely that it is the same bridge throughout, and that this famous structure may have been built in the C13th.

There was also once a tiny chapel at the centre of the bridge (this can be seen on some old engravings) where a bible clerk, Cuthbert Hilton, performed illicit weddings for half-a-crown. During the great floods of 1771 great damage was done to the bridge and the chapel disappeared as rebuilding work took place. The date '1596 ER' which is carved into the bridge is a C19th rebuilding error. At the southern end of the bridge can be seen the ancient 'White Swan Inn' one of the oldest and most interesting of the town's hostelries on what was once the Yorkshire side of the river, whilst along the river bank are relics of the former woollen, carpet and leather industries for which the town had a wide reputation. Thorngate Mill stands as a reminder of these times. Here can be seen many fine old buildings such as the Weaver's Cottages next to the mills and the grand Georgian 'Thorngate House'. Thorngate leads back to The Bank and the Market Cross where at the junction with Newgate is the plaque marking the former site of the shop of Thomas Humphreys, the subject of Charles Dickens' story, 'Master Humphrey's Clock'.

As a centre to visit Barnard Castle certainly has much to offer.

THE
WHITE SWAN INN

BRIDGE END,
STARTFORTH, BARNARD CASTLE
Tel: TEESDALE 37575

15th Century Ale House
situated on the river in the shadow
of the castle.

Fresh cut Sandwiches and home-made
Bar meals served
every lunch time and night.

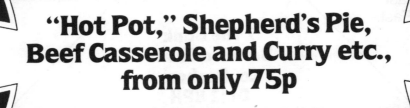

**"Hot Pot," Shepherd's Pie,
Beef Casserole and Curry etc.,
from only 75p**

Children Welcome

Tea and Coffee on request

RABY ARMS HOTEL

17 MARKET PLACE, BARNARD CASTLE
TELEPHONE: (0833) 37105
(under new management)

Personal Service from the Godden Family.

Open to non-residents.

· · · ● · · ·

Free House · Residential · Restaurant

· · · ● · · ·

Bar meals, Sunday lunch, Parties catered for.

· · · ● · · ·

Bed and Breakfast.

· · · ● · · ·

Tea & coffee making facilities and colour T.V.'s in all rooms.

· · · ● · · ·

Evening meal available in the restaurant, residents bar.

· · · ● · · ·

Car Park at the rear · Children and dogs welcome.

· · · ● · · ·

Theakstons and Camerons Ales.

Middleton-in-Teesdale is often referred to as the natural centre and capital of Upper Teesdale. This large village is found in a very pretty setting on the north bank of the River Tees where it is joined by the beautiful wooded valley of the Hudeshope Beck. As one approaches Middleton-in-Teesdale it can be seen nestling on the green, wooded rural valley floor below the steep valley slopes and the high Pennine Fells.

Possessing many of the characteristics of the dalesfolk themselves, it has not bowed to commercialism as have villages in other tourist areas of the country. As a result Middleton-in-Teesdale with its resolute and practical character may not really be described as a 'typical model village', though this has proved to be both an advantage and an attraction. Its stone buildings of various ages and style combine well with the tall trees of the village green to make this a most picturesque centre of interest for the visitor to the area.

The environs of Middleton were inhabited at an early date, hence Kirkcarrion and Swinkley Knoll (see 'Early Settlers'). But the village itself is probably of Saxon or Viking origin. It is first mentioned as being part of Staindropshire and owned by King Canute about 1030, although by 1093 it was granted to the Baliols along with Gainford and the forests of Marwood and Teesdale.

The oldest remnant of the past in Middleton is probably the base of the Cross on Seed Hill now surmounted by a sundial. This may have served as a preaching point before the first church was built.

This event occurred before 1160 when the Baliols gave the chapel at Middleton, dependant on the mother church at Gainford, to the abbey of St. Mary's York, the most famous abbey of Black Benedictine monks in the North. Tomb lids from this early period and later can be found built into the north wall of the present church (for keys to the church see Rev. G. Linden, The Rectory, Hude). The chapel later became a church (about 1240) with a Rector and was probably totally rebuilt in the C13th. The fine decorated window in the churchyard is of this church. Added about 1557 was the detached belfry which still can be seen to the west of the church. Reverend William Bell presented a bell to the church at that time which can also be viewed. The belfry is the only such bell tower in County Durham.

Of the streets of Middleton, Hude is

mentioned about 1200 and the Hill occurs in the early C14th. It may be that the area around Hude, the Mill and the chapel, was the earliest focus for a settlement.

At any rate the village green allowed cattle to be brought into the centre for protection at night and then out through the garths of the cottages along the 'back way' to the common fields.

The Old Rectory, which can be seen from the churchyard, was rebuilt in the C17th and C18th and includes some medieval work.

Other old farmhouses include Stotley Hall, 1½ miles from Middleton on the Eggleston Road. It was built in C17th with mullioned windows of the period, but a farm existed there in 1220. It was separate from the field systems of Middleton with its own manor courts and hunting rights.

Some Georgian buildings exist including the Working Men's Club (formerly the Rose and Crown Inn). Two hotels reflect landownership in the dale - the former Cleveland Arms (now the Teesdale Hotel), for the Duke of Cleveland was once the title of Lord Barnard, and the Talbot Hotel, being the first name of a number of the Bowes family.

But the biggest changes in the village were to come when the London Lead Company arrived on the scene. After fifty years in the dale having acquired leases of lead mines from the Duke of Cleveland, they bought up an estate in Middleton in 1815, and began their gradual process of transforming the village. They built Masterman Place (1823) and New Town, giving the best houses to those they considered most deserving. A reading room was erected in Masterman Place (1854) and there was a free library of over 1000 volumes. A Ready Money Shop and a Corn Association (1842) were started, the latter seen as the beginning of the Co-operative Movement in Teesdale.

On Hude, the Clock Tower with weighbridge, lead yard and stables, Middleton House and the Grove were all the work of the "Company". Middleton House became the headquarters of the whole company after 1880.

The Quaker owned company were very keen on the social welfare of their workforce. They built schools, the first on Hude (1819) and then the one that can still be seen on Alston Road (1861). These were ahead of their time, but conflict arose with the Bishop of Durham over whether in fact they were 'Church Schools'.

The Company also ran Evening Classes and set up a Mechanics Institute in the building then known as the Town Hall but today known as The 'Mechanics'.

The health of the workforce was also a high priority. They had their own doctors and also appointed an assistant who received £300 and £70 per year respectively. The Company provided public washhouses and perhaps even a bath house. It gave to its workers a large garden in which to grow vegetables and some of the gardens even had pig-sties attached. It helped set up horticultural societies, brass bands, and mechanic institutes.

The Company was also keen to encourage the religious activities in the dale, although it did not set up a Quaker Meeting House in Middleton. Its workforce was expected to attend some place of worship every Sunday and there were at least four from which to chose. The Baptist Chapel on Hude (1827) is still standing; The Wesleyan Methodist Chapel (now the Methodist Church) 1870; the Primitive Methodist Chapel (now an artist's studio) 1872; and the Anglican Church rebuilt about 1878. There were earlier Methodist chapels; in fact the first meeting house is said to be on the site of Middleton House. During these early days, John Wesley visited Teesdale 10 times on his horse. On one of his later visits in 1784 the people heard him 'with gladness' but it had not always been so.

Two other features of the village are its arches, in particular the decorative arch in Masterman Place which originally had its gates shut by a certain time at night (a curfew); and also the decorative cast iron fountain erected in 1877 to commemorate a testimonial given to Robert Bainbridge by London Lead Company employees. Bainbridge was the company superintendent. His grave can be seen in the churchyard. So can that of Richard Watson, the Teesdale poet, whose poetry sprang from his love of Teesdale, and from the hard life of the miners.

The Company pulled out of Teesdale in 1905. New buildings since then include the Infant and Junior School, The Roman Catholic Church, The Village Hall, and the New Surgery. Another building to note is the old town hall built by the former Duke of Cleveland. Sadly it has lost most of its former grandeur. Also to be seen, are the two old mills which stand as testimony to those not-too-distant days of water power, whilst reminders of the era of horse-drawn carriages are the stone-archways of the village inns and hotels.

Apart from its own features of interest Middleton-in-Teesdale is centred in an area of great wealth. By using the information in this guide one can enjoy not only the riches of nature but also the beauty spots, historical sites, picnic sites, drives, walks and sporting activities, all of which are found in this Teesdale area of the High Pennines.

Middleton-in-Teesdale(SR)

The ancient church window(MP)

Bowes

At first glance the small village of Bowes, which is situated beside the busy A66(T), may not seem much of a centre to visit. However, we must not be fooled. Not only is the countryside surrounding Bowes most varied and very beautiful but there is also a wealth of history to be unfolded. Bowes is situated in the Stainmore Gap which has been a major routeway between the west and east of England for thousands of years. The history of this Pass and the village of Bowes go hand in hand. The name Bowes is thought by some to originate from a bend in the River Greta.

During the Norman conquest, William the Conqueror made Alan Niger, Earl of Richmond. To protect his lands of Richmond his successors built a tower within the site of the old Roman fort of Lavatrae at Bowes. This fort is described in greater detail elsewhere. Being on a hill it was quite a good vantage point to look out for marauding Scots venturing over Stainmore. The castle itself is a single Norman keep of three storeys surrounded by a deep ditch. It is unique in that it is possibly the only instance of a rectangular Norman keep built about 1170 AD which is still unconnected to any other buildings.

The castle was besieged in 1173 by William the Lion, King of Scotland, who was attempting to make the whole of the four northern counties subject to him.

Another siege occurred in 1322 when Henry Fitz Hugh, who had probably lost his castle at Cotherstone in Scots raids which had left it devastated, decided to besiege Bowes and proceeded to take it while the Earl of Richmond was in Parliament, but the Earl eventually got it back. There are a number of myths relating to Bowes castle, such as 'When Julius Caeser ruled a king, Bowes Castle was a famous thing' which mixes up the Roman and Medieval periods, and the tradition that Alan placed it in the charge of his brother, William, and left him 500 archers. It is said that William assumed the surname 'de Arcubus' which is Latin for bows. 500 archers is an impossible number at this time, and in any case the tower was not built yet. It is also said that not only was the village named after him but that he was an ancestor of the Bowes family of Streatlam, the predecessors of the Earls of Strathmore from whom our present Royal Family is descended. The origin of the name Bowes was long held by the family to have come from Bows used in archery and there may be some truth in this, although the story as a whole must have become exaggerated.

Sadly the castle suffered so much from the attentions of the Scots that by 1340 it was reported to be in poor condition and worth nothing.

Centuries passed and Stainmore saw many important events including the "Wars of the Roses" and the 'Rising of the North'. Later, Stainmore became a major routeway for horse-drawn coaches. In fact, on Wednesday, 31st January, 1838, Charles Dickens arrived by coach at Greta Bridge and, after a short stay in Barnard Castle, he arrived at the 'Unicorn Inn', a well-known coaching inn which may still be found today at Bowes. It was here that Dickens met William Shaw and saw his Academy. They became famous as Mr. Squeers and Dotheboys Hall in his novel 'Nicholas Nickleby'. The 'Dotheboys Hall' of Dickens can still be seen at the western end of the village and in the churchyard are buried Shaw and some of his pupils. This churchyard is of the Church of St. Giles which was probably built by the Normans at about the same time as the castle. However, it has been rebuilt at certain times in its history, though traces of the original building still remain. It offers much of interest to the visitor.

The oldest parts to survive are two Norman doorways, the C14th transepts, and early C15th carved stone over the south porch showing the crucifixion of Christ; a Norman font standing on a Roman altar; and another Roman inscribed stone in the interior. The church was heavily restored in 1864 and much of the rest is modern. The church originally stood within the castle walls, and was granted by the Earls to the Hospital of St. Peter of York.

Linked to this church is the story of Mallet's ballad, published in 1760, entitled 'Edwin and Emma'. Tradition has it that Rodger Wrightson and Martha Railton, both from Bowes, were young lovers. Sadly Rodger caught a fever and died and within a few hours on that same day, March 15th, 1714, Martha died of a broken heart. They were buried in the same grave, which, according to legend, lies at the western end of the church below the bells which had tolled Rodger's passing. In 1848 near this spot Doctor Dinsdale erected a monument to their memory. Local tradition has it that the 'Unicorn Inn' is also linked to this tale because it is thought that this building was originally the 'George Inn' where Martha lived with her mother who was landlady there.

Today, with such a wealth of attractions, Bowes receives many visitors.

The Castle Hotel, Brough, Cumbria.
(Tel: 093 04 252)

A luxury hotel in a quiet and secluded Westmorland Village. Convenient for the main A66.

All bedrooms have bathroom facilities en-suite, colour television, telephone, radio/alarm and tea/coffee making facilities.

Separate restaurant open to non-residents.

Bar snacks, Table d'hote and A la Carte.

Lounge bar and public bar.

Separate residents' lounge.

Ample private parking.

Explore a fragment of Eden, Herriott Country, Wordsworth Country and the land of the Prince Bishops

Brough

The green, rural landscape of the Upper Eden Valley, nestling beneath the lofty peaks of the Pennine's western scarp, is one steeped in history and tradition. Here we feature upon an area centred on the small, stone-built country towns, such as Brough, and dispersed farmsteads and cottages that comprise of the settlements known as North and South Stainmore.

It may seem strange that such a remote and sparsely-populated area should today, as indeed it was in the past, be regarded as being of great importance. However, we must not forget that it lies on one of the very few east-west trans-Pennine routeways in Northern England.

The almost impenetrable barrier of the rugged Pennine Hills has always been a problem to travellers, yet here amidst some of the highest Pennine peaks is found a pass attaining a meagre maximum height of 447 metres (1468 feet) above sea-level and at a point where the Pennines narrow to only 16 miles.

Nevertheless, despite these obvious advantages, the winter months make these wide expanses of moorland a very lonely place and indeed impassable during heavy falls of snow and severe drifting.

The first traveller through the Stainmore Gap was the Stainmore Glacier. During the Ice-Age the Eden Valley was filled with ice from glaciers flowing down from the surrounding hills. Eventually, the level of ice rose to a point where it overflowed into the Stainmore Gap as the Stainmore Glacier, which travelled eastward towards the North Sea. When the climate became warmer and the ice melted, the pass was covered with clay and boulders that had once been carried in the ice. It is from this stone-covered moorland or 'stony moor' that Stainmore derived its name.

As the climate became warmer the ice melted and, shortly after, Stone-Age man ventured north. He and his descendants, Bronze-Age man and Iron-Age man, used the Stainmore Gap as a major routeway. A stone battle-axe and a bronze axe found at Bowes are evidence of their presence, as is the huge circular hill fort at Stanwick St. John which is thought to have been built by the Brigantes in an unsuccessful attempt to stop the Roman Advance.

The Romans did advance in AD79 under the leadership of General Julius Agricola. Eventually they built a road, the Iter II from Scotland, Carlisle, Penrith and Brough across the pass to Bowes, Catterick and York, and a branch road to the east through Barnard Castle to Binchester, whilst another to the west climbed over Melmerby Fell passing Alston on the way to the Roman Wall. Protecting the roads were a series of Roman Forts such as Whitley Castle near Alston, Verterae at Brough, Maiden Castle on Stainmore Summit, Lavatrae at Bowes and others further east at Greta Bridge and Piercebridge.

Verterae at Brough guarded the western end of the Stainmore Pass, whilst Lavatrae at Bowes guarded its eastern end. This latter fort covered a 1.6 hectare (4 acre) site enclosing the present Norman castle, church, churchyard and vicarage, and also had the luxury of baths for the garrison. Water was channelled by aquaduct from the Levy pool in the Deepdale Beck over 2 miles (3km) to the north-west. During the final decline of the Roman Empire in the C4th this fort was the last single outpost on the northern frontier, before it too was abandoned. Many Roman remains have been found in the area to the present day and include coins, jewellery, pottery and inscriptions.

In the centuries that followed Stainmore saw the passage of many settlers from other lands, including the Vikings. Rey Cross, found near the summit of Stainmore within the old Roman Camp, was erected by King Edmund before 946 AD to mark the boundary between Scottish Cumberland and his English Kingdom of Northumbria.

Much later, following the Norman invasion and the 'harrying of the North' in an attempt to remove final Northern resistance to their rule, a series of castles were built. Another reason for their construction was the realisation that it was one thing winning the area, but it was another holding it. They had to frequently resist the forays of marauding Scots venturing south of the border intent on plunder. Castles were built, once again at either end of the pass, one of these being at Brough, whose impressive remains are open to the public.

Dating from the C11th, Brough castle is built upon the site of the Roman fort known as Verterae. Obviously the Normans, just like the Romans some 1000 years before, had viewed this location as being of great strategic importance. The Romans had wished to protect the western approaches to their major road over Stainmore to York from Carlisle, whilst King William II wished to protect his acquired lands of North Westmorland, Cumberland and Carlisle by the construction of this castle about 1092. Until 1204, when it was given to Robert de Vipont, an ancestor of the powerful Clifford Family, by King John, it was a Royal castle.

Much of the earliest C11th fabric remains, but there have been many alterations over the centuries. Much of this was rebuilding work being necessitated by the attentions of the Scots. In 1174 King William, the Lion of Scotland, demolished much of the original structure, and after restoration it was again in a poor state of repair by the mid-C13th. Obviously, this restoration did nothing to stop the repeated Scottish raids, but the rebuilt castle, now much stronger, became a safe place of refuge for the inhabitants of the area. Sadly, for them, the Scots turned their attentions to the village. In the August of 1314, and again in 1329, the Scots burnt and destroyed the village and surrounding farmsteads, whilst all the local people could do was watch from their refuge. Further building work was undertaken by Robert, the 1st Lord Clifford, and Roger, the 5th Lord Clifford, in the early and late C14th.

Later, in the 'Wars of the Roses', John the 9th Lord Clifford, also known as 'The Butcher' or 'Bloody Clifford', was killed in battle in 1461. The castle then became a possession of the Warwick Family, namely 'Warwick the Kingmaker', before eventually becoming a Clifford possession once again. Sadly, during a Christmas feast, an enormous accidental fire left the building as a ruin. So it remained until 1662, when Lady Anne Clifford completed restoration work.

But the life of the castle was coming to a close. Towards the end of the C17th the keep had been damaged and much of its stone 'quarried' for use as a building stone elsewhere, in places such as Appleby. The fittings of the castle were removed and sold in 1714, Clifford's Tower was largely dismantled to repair Brough Mill in 1763, the south-east section of the keep collapsed in 1792, and the south-western corner did the same in 1920...such a sad decline! Today, standing prominent on an escarpment above the Swindale Beck, the substantial and impressive ruins are in the care of English Heritage and are certainly well worth a visit.

The view from the lofty perch at the top of the ruined keep is really breathtaking. On the one hand there is the western escarpment of the mighty Pennine Hills, whilst on the other hand, below is the ruined courtyard and castle buildings and the small settlement of Church Brough, the original village.

The present village of Brough developed a little later, when the routeway across the Pennines began to use a better bridging point across the Swindale Beck, a short distance to the north of Church Brough. This bridging point became a centre of trade, and the resulting present settlement, sometimes referred to as 'Market Brough', was born. So busy was this village that it was granted its Charter by King Edward III in 1330, with a weekly market being held every Thursday and a fair every September.

However, with the arrival of the railways, road transport declined and so did the prosperity of the markets and fair. This resulted in the end of the weekly market in 1867, but the tradition of the Brough Hill Fair continues. Every year, in September, farmers, countryfolk and travelling people make their way here to trade as well as enjoy a major social event on the calendar. Walking through Brough today, it is possible to imagine the market stalls and pens of livestock lining the wide main street which served as testimony to this journey back in time.

Two other traditions which have now disappeared were the mid-winter fire-festival held on the eve of Epiphany to encourage the rebirth of the waning sun, and the existence, until the 1960s, oa town crier. But one piece of history that does still exist is the old Norman church whose structure largely dates from the C14th-C16th. This fine old building possesses a 'leper's squint' and an inscribed stone from the Roman fort recording its rebuilding in 197 AD.

A recent attraction in the area is the Dyke Nook Farm Museum which is conveniently located beside the A66 at Warcop, which is only a few miles north of Brough. Although still in its development there is still certainly much to interest the visitor. As well as a collection of vintage farm machinery there is a variety of farm animals including Shire and Clydesdale horses. Steam threshing can also be seen on occasions...and for that family day out, there is even a picnic area.

Stainmore, Brough and the Upper Eden Valley not only has a wealth of beauty, history and interest, but also provides an excellent base for exploring the High Pennines, the Yorkshire Dales and the Lake District.

THE
GRAND PRIX
CLUB
Brough
ENTERTAINMENT

Music – Dancing – Restaurant – Bar Meals.
A wide range of music and entertainment
for all ages and tastes.

LEISURE CENTRE

Squash Courts, Solarium, Exercise Room (Weight Training), Table Tennis, Badminton, Indoor Bowls, Tennis, Volley Ball, Basket Ball, 5 a side football.

For details and bookings simply telephone:

Brough (09304) 517/328

MOSS &
CAMPBELL
FURNITURE &
DIVAN CENTRES

Large selection of 3-PIECE SUITES and all types of CHAIRS, BACK CARE RECLINER, ROCKERS, HIGH SEATS, etc.

DINING ROOM FURNITURE.

BEDROOM FURNITURE.

DIVANS, MATTRESSES, BUNK BEDS, etc. All sizes available.

OCCASIONAL TABLES, NESTS, TROLLEYS, TV AND HI FI CABINETS, BOOKCASES, etc.

PICTURES, MIRRORS, ORNAMENTAL LAMPS AND FIRESIDE RUGS.

Most goods available from stock.   Barclaycard/Access, etc

Up to £1,500 instant credit subject to status APR 29.9%

Credit brokers. Written details on request.

MOSS & CAMPBELL
28 GALGATE, BARNARD CASTLE. Tel: Teesdale (0833) 31555
321-324 NORTH ROAD, DARLINGTON Tel: (0325) 482333

DISCOVER
EDEN DISTRICT

Discover the delights of this most beautiful part of Cumbria. You will find the district makes an ideal base for exploring the unspoilt countryside, the valleys and fells. To the west of the M6 lies (Ullswater, perhaps the most beautiful of all the lakes and a few miles to the south, Haweswater in peaceful seclusion. To the east of the M6 lies the delightful Eden Valley with its changing scenery which is second to none. To the north east of the district discover the tranquillity of Alston Moor and the Pennine Fells.

Whichever part of the district you choose you will find much to see and do – the market towns of Penrith, Alston, Appleby and Kirkby Stephen – the stately homes of Hutton-in-the Forest and Dalemain – Lowther Wildlife Park – the South Tynedale Railway at Alston – Penrith Steam Museum – Castles – churches – these are just a few of the many attractions which Eden has to offer.

Eden District has an extensive range of accommodation to suit all tastes. For a free Tourist information Pack and Accommodation Guide send to the address below.

Tourist Information Centre, Robinson's School, Middlegate, Penrith, Cumbria CA11 7QF.
Telephone Penrith (0768) 67466 or 64671

Indoor and Outdoor

LEISURE IN PENRITH

The many facilities available in the attractive surroundings of Castle Park include Tennis, Bowling, Putting, Childrens Play equipment, Paddling Pool and of course refreshments.

Be sure to discover our modern 25-Metre heated Swimming Pool, Solarium Sauna Suite and fitness room at Southend Road.

enjoy your visit to Penrith
... enjoy your leisure.

Eden
District
Council

Kirkby Stephen & The Upper Eden Valley

Known as the capital of Upper Eden, Kirkby Stephen has for centuries been an important settlement in the Eden Valley. At about 600 feet (180 metres) above sea level, it is the highest town on the Eden, and is an important stopping place for travellers.

Kirkby is predominantly an agricultural town and regular auction marts are held here. Hill sheep are perhaps the biggest commodities passing through the mart, but cattle sales are also held. For the odd half hour or so on Market day, it is well worth dropping in to the mart and watching the farmers transacting their business as they have done for centuries.

The town is believed to have been formed in Anglo-Saxon and Norse times and there is certainly some evidence to substantiate that. In the church there is a carved stone of Viking origin, and the name of the town is also Viking. But the town may have begun earlier; the original church in the town was of Saxon construction, and close to the town are several cultivation terraces or lynchets of Saxon origin.

The church has C13th Early English arcades and a C15th south aisle. The tombs of the Wharton family of Wharton Hall are found here, as are the medieval tombs of Andrew de Harck, executed by Edward II, and Sir Richard Musgrave, who is said to have killed the last wild boar in England · he was buried with the boar's tusk.

The long main street and the Market Place dominate the centre of the town, whose original market charter dates from 1351. To the side of the Market Place are a series of cloisters which lead to the church lawn. Many of the buildings around the Market Place are of architectural interest and it is unusual to see so many different styles in such a close area.

The long main street through the town, it is nearly a mile long, gives the impression that the town is larger than it is. In fact the town has very little width and most of the buildings are clustered tightly side by side along the main street. The Eden flows to the east of the town and on the banks of the river there are the remains of a pele tower. The Eden is flanked by pastures as it passes close by the town and the town's agricultural links are seen when walking along the riverside path beside the Eden.

One of the ways to reach the Eden is along a narrow alleyway from the Market Place. At the riverside a narrow C17th bridge is found. The quaint footbridge is known locally as Franks Bridge and is well known to photographers and artists alike.

Stenkrith Park, which is reached from the Nateby Road, lies close to the site of the old North Eastern Railway Company's station in the town and borders on the River Eden. From Stenkrith Bridge, the Eden swirls down a series of limestone pavings and small waterfalls. The water has worn fissures and circular depressions in the rock and here the river bed is like so many of the famous rivers in the Yorkshire Dales. One of the places along the river here is known locally as 'The Devil's Mustard Mill', due to the machinery like noises that the swirling waters create. The park is well known and loved by local people, but nevertheless it is very quiet and tranquil. Bird life is abundant and occasionally wild life may also be seen.

Railways played an important part in the development of the town. At the far end of the town was a station on the Midland Railway's line to Scotland. Though no scheduled services on the Settle-Carlisle stop at Kirkby Stephen Station today, the platforms are maintained by Cumbria County Council and the Dales Rail service operates summer trains which stop at the town.

Closer to the town is the site of the North Eastern Railway's station. The line which came over Stainmore reached the town by a spectacular descent which included the magnificent tubular steel viaduct over the River Belah. Beyond the town the line split and the main line ran to a junction with the West Coast Main Line at Tebay. A minor line curved away to the north to Warcop and Penrith.

Today, coaches carry the majority of visitors to the town; it is an important stopping place on the route of excursion coaches from the North East to the Southern Lakes and Lancashire. The service coach from Newcastle to Morecambe and Blackpool stops in the town and several others use the town for a lunch stop; a fact which explains the predominance of cafes and restaurants which can be found within the town.

The town is an ideal centre for walkers and hikers. There is an excellent Youth Hostel right in the main street, and recently a specialist hikers shop was opened here.

Above the town are the Nine Standards which sit on the brow of a hill about 650 metres (2150 ft) above sea level. The Nine Standards are a series of nine stone-built cairns of gigantic proportions, and in honesty no one knows who built them or why. The hill has become known as Nine Standards and a little further along is Nine Standards Rigg; there has been considerable conjecture as to who, when and why! One theory is that they were erected as boundary markers, a common enough practice throughout the north, but usually single cairns are raised at regular intervals. Furthermore, the Standards are some distance from the actual county boundary which has remained unchanged at this point for centuries. As the cairns are visible on the hill crest for some considerable distance, it has been suggested that they were built to delude possible Scottish raiders into thinking that an English army was encamped there. They are of some considerable antiquity and this is undisputed. Sir Walter Scott referred to them in his 'Bridal of Trierman' and they are found mentioned on maps dating from as long ago as the early 1700s.

From the town of Kirkby Stephen we move to the villages of the Upper Eden Valley.

The Upper Eden Valley strictly covers the whole of the upper end of the vale including Stainmore, Brough, Kirkby Stephen and the Mallerstang. We have endeavoured to describe some of the villages elsewhere that are not described within this book. To define the area we have described as the Upper Eden, we have followed the course of the river from the outskirts of Kirkby Stephen to Warcop.

Though little visited, the area between Kirkby Stephen and Warcop is most picturesque. The river now begins to grow in importance with the addition of water contributed by the River Belah and the Swindale and Scandal Becks.

The first village reached after the Eden leaves Kirkby Stephen is Winton, just off the A685 about a mile and a half from the town. The village is built up around a triangular shaped green. Winton Hall, built in the C17th is now in a very poor condition. In 1726, the Georgian style manor house was built and in its past once served as a boys boarding school. At the far end of the village, Jill Cookson operates Langrigg Pottery and welcomes visitors to her workshops. The nearby inn serves meals on pottery made at Langrigg.

Due west of Winton lies Soulby, a romantic little village with the attractive Scandal Beck

running right through its centre. Wide open farm lands hereabouts contrast dramatically with places like Mallerstang and Stainmore, and it is probably at this point where the Vale of Eden takes up a face that follows it down towards the sea.

Down river from Soulby and near the confluence of the Eden and Swindale Beck are the villages of Little Musgrave and Great Musgrave. Little Musgrave is obviously the smaller of the two and lies across the river from its larger neighbour. The river between the villages is spanned by a fine sandstone bridge of two arches. Great Musgrave has an unusual tourist attraction for it still follows the tradition of rush-bearing. This ancient tradition is one that has been practiced since medieval times and is thought by some historians to have its origins in pagan practices. The rush-bearing service is held annually in the village. Originally it was an event where rushes were gathered to cover the church floor, today it is a parade of local children wearing crowns of flowers on their heads. Following the parade to the church, a service is read and the crowns are hung in the church. Afterwards there are a series of sports, games and picnic type refreshments.

The last of the villages covered in this section is Warcop, home to a large Ministry of Defence (Army) establishment and artillery range. A section of the old railway line which ran from Kirkby Stephen to Penrith is still intact to Appleby for the movement of Military traffic.

Despite a considerable army presence, the village is quite untainted, it has regularly entered, and won awards in the area's Best Kept Village competition. The Eden flows shallow but wide here, and on a fine summers evening you can sit along the river banks and wander back in time lazily watching the trout jumping and the more energetic trying to catch them. Through the village runs a quaint mill stream and the village green is a delight. Close to Warcop is Dyke Nook Farm, a working farm with a farm museum attached. Visitors to the area should not fail to visit the museum which is a delight to both young and old alike.

2 miles south of Brough is the village of Kaber originally owned by a family of that name. Its only claim to fame is the so called Kaber Rigg Plot devised by those who were displeased at the restoration of Charles II in 1660. The leader of the plot, Captain Appleby, was unfortunately beheaded for his part in it.

Appleby

Appleby takes its name from the Vikings who settled here in the C10th. But near the end of the C11th the Normans began to influence the development of the town. King William Rufus, on his march north to Carlisle, established Ranulph de Meshines as the lord of the lands within the Eden Valley. Ranulph built castles or fortifications at Brougham, Brough and Appleby. The land in the valley was still claimed by Malcolm III, so it is not surprising that there were considerable disturbances in the area around this time.

The castle at Appleby was built on a hill rising above a loop in the river. This loop of the river made a natural moat and so the site was an ideal place for a fortification. Its most famous siege was in 1174 when William the Lion, King of Scotland, took it because, one source says, it was left unguarded. Despite the formidable fort that was built here the next two centuries saw the continuation of Border warfare.

Appleby was made a Royal Burgh in 1174 and Henry II granted a charter to the town in 1179. The town grew in size and several pre-reformation religious orders were established in the area. A leper colony is believed to have caused some problems for the town in the C13th and so the leper hospital of St. Leonard was built on the northern outskirts of Appleby. In 1388 one of the worst ever raids on the town took place and much of the town was left burning. In 1598 the town suffered the effects of the plague and a number of burial sites of plague victims can be traced.

In the Civil War, the town adhered to the Royalist Cause and the Roundhead garrison of the town proved unpopular. With the return of Charles II, there were great celebrations. Lady Anne Clifford, when she took possession of her estates in 1643, began a massive restoration programme which included the repair of her castles at Skipton and Bardon in Yorkshire, and Pendragon, Brough, Brougham and Appleby in the Eden Valley.

The Borough of Appleby reached its peak during the later Middle Ages. It originally had great walls but the decline in trade, and the Scots raids, caused it to languish. In the time of William and Mary it was said to have been in ruins. But it did revive later and there was considerable industry.

Some of the old builings around the town show their past use, try walking around the town to find the Bobbin Mill, the Corset Factory, the Old Brewery or any of the old mills. One such mill is situated off Bondgate, on the banks of the Eden where a ford and footbridge cross the river. Bondgate Mill was originally used for milling but today houses a pottery and craft workshop.

Fairs and markets have been important to the people of the town and the surrounding area for many past centuries. A market charter was granted to Appleby by King John and still continues to this day. Originally the market was for the sale of grain, provisions and produce, but today a wide variety of goods are to be found on sale.

In the town centre can be found the Moot Hall, some 400 years old, the centre of local government and the meeting place for the Town Council. In one of the shops below the building is the Tourist Information Centre from where visitors can obtain information they require about the town. There are several sites that are worth seeing whilst in the town. Jack Robinson's house (he is remembered in the children's nursery rhyme 'The House that Jack Built!') can be seen in Boroughgate. At the bottom of the Boroughgate is the Market Place, with the cloisters set along the bottom side, where every Saturday a market is held.

The riverside is a pleasant place to wander and watch the fish jumping, or to pause a while alongside the cricket ground. A small park is set on the side of the hill between the Sands and Garth Head road and provides an attractive short cut for pedestrians to reach the railway station which is set high above the town. There were two medieval parish churches in Appleby . St. Lawrence's and St. Michael's. The second parish was known as Bondgate because the bond tenants of the borough lived there. The two churches have much of interest. St. Laurence's was originally owned by the Benedictine Abbey of St. Mary's, York.

For those with a little energy, the town is an ideal centre for recreation; the open-air, heated swimming pool is open to the public from May to mid-October; cricket and football clubs are found in the town; bowls may be played at the bowling club located off The Sands where non-members are welcome; golf can be played on the scenic course at Brackenber Moor where an 18 hole course provides a challenge to the visitor; fishing is plentiful on the River Eden and its tributaries and permits may be obtained in the town centre. A guide to a series of quiet walks around Appleby can be obtained from the information centre.

Places to Picnic

Many of the visitors coming to Teesdale and this extremely beautiful part of the High Pennines enjoy having a good old-fashioned picnic. However, perhaps on reflection I'm being a little unfair in saying 'old-fashioned' because the excitement and pleasure that can be generated in the planning, preparation and participation in such an adventure may be enormous, and as a result the family picnic will probably always remain popular.

However, there is one problem facing the would-be 'adventurer': this is finding a site suitable for a picnic. Some may simply trust to luck to find a picnic-site whenever they feel hungry, but this can be far from ideal as many of you will know. How often have you seen people picnicking on the roadside verges next to the noisy and dangerous traffic? How often have you seen a really suitable site whilst you have been driving through the area? Of course some of you will explore the countryside to find one, but there is one thing to remember: you could be on private property and guilty of trespass. Always obtain permission from the landowner. Anyway I believe the majority of people like to have some idea of where they are going before they set off. Therefore I have increased their choice by offering several possible locations, outlined below. (An entrance fee may be payable at some of these sites but they do tend to have extra facilities and benefits).

The Bowlees Picnic Area is found in the hamlet of Bowlees about 3 miles (4km) west of Middleton-in-Teesdale and a short distance to the north of the B6277. This site, which was developed by Durham County Council with grant-aid from the Countryside Commission, has much to offer the visitor. It is away from the main road in the secluded, peaceful, wooded valley of the Flushiemere Beck. In fact, this picturesque little stream has formed several small waterfalls as it meanders through the picnic site. There are also facilities such as car parks, picnic and play areas, and toilets. However, certain rules must be observed. These include; follow the country code; don't fish in the beck; don't light fires; and keep away from the quarry face which could prove dangerous.

The site has other attractions, such as the short walk of about 500 metres along the beck-side to the beautiful Summerhill Force Waterfall with Gibson's Cave behind it. This walk is not a public right of way as it is on land belonging to the Raby Estates; however, permission for

public access has kindly been given by them.

Another attraction is the indoor Durham County Conservation Trust's Visitors' Centre which has been established in a converted chapel only about 100 metres from the car park. Here the visitor can learn more about Teesdale at both his leisure and pleasure. Two final attractions, Wynch Bridge and the Low Force Waterfall, can be reached by a short, 500 metre walk to the north bank of the River Tees.

Durham County Council have developed another site only about 3 miles from Bowlees and 6 miles west of Middleton-in-Teesdale. This is the small, near-roadside, possibly 'short-stay' halt known as Hanging Shaw which, because of the many nearby public footpaths, is often used as a base by walkers. It has fine views south of the Tees Valley to Cronkley Scar and White Force Waterfall.

Between Bowlees and Hanging Shaw is another picnic site, this one belonging to the Raby Estates. This is the High Force Car Park which has picnic and toilet facilities and occupies quite a large site. An added attraction is the wooded walk to the famous High Force Waterfall. Adjacent to this site is the 'High Force Hotel' which can offer refreshments and has a small shop where ices and soft drinks may be purchased.

The Raby Estates also provide another area where picnicking is available. This is in the grounds of one of the most magnificent medieval castles in the country - Raby Castle at Staindrop. The parkland around the castle is very beautiful and it is possible to see sheep, cattle and even herds of deer grazing upon it. There are other advantages of this site with the extensive gardens, coach houses and of course the castle itself along with its splendid contents.

In Barnard Castle are the magnificent building and collections of Bowes Museum where visitors are allowed to enjoy their lunches in the beautiful grounds and gardens. Nearby is that riverside grassland known as the Desmesnes, which, though relatively secluded, is very near to the town and its attractions and services.

A specialist picnic area is that of Whorlton Lido. This is situated on the south bank of the River Tees in the green and rural valley near the village of Whorlton 4 miles (7km) downstream and east of Barnard Castle. This is

KILLHOPE WHEEL
LEAD MINING CENTRE

UPPER WEARDALE, COUNTY DURHAM
(alongside A689, 2½ miles west of Cowshill)

**The most complete surviving lead mining site in
Britain. A dramatic setting high up in the Pennine
dales. Learn how lead was mined and processed,
and about the harsh life of the miners and their families.**

**Pan for lead, work the machines the miners used,
pump the blacksmith's bellows — you can get
involved with the action at Killhope.**

**OPEN DAILY 10.30 a.m. - 5.00 p.m.
APRIL — END OF OCTOBER**

DURHAM COUNTY COUNCIL
PLANNING DEPARTMENT

RABY CASTLE
(The Seat of the Lord Barnard, TD)

Staindrop, Nr. Darlington
Off A688 Barnard Castle – Bishop Auckland
Magnificent Mediaeval castle, fully
furnished, with fine pictures and
porcelain. Splendid 14th century Great
Kitchen and Servants' Hall. Collection of
Carriages and Horse-drawn vehicles.
Walled Gardens

OPENING HOURS 1987
Easter Saturday-Wednesday
May 2nd – 30th September
May and June – Weds and Sundays only
July – September – daily except Saturdays
Castle open 1-5 p.m.
Park and Gardens open – 11 a.m.-5.30 p.m.
Last admission 4.30 p.m.

Parties welcome on other days by
appointment. Tearooms and Souvenir
Shops. Car and Coach Parking. Picnic
tables adjacent Car Park
For further information telephone Curator,
Staindrop (0833) 60202

LANGLEY CASTLE
**Langley on Tyne
near Hexham**

14th Century Castle now magnificently
restored to a fine Country Hotel. Eight
Bedrooms, each with en-suite bathroom
and individually appointed to the highest
of standards, are complimented by a first
class Restaurant (open to non-residents),
elegant Drawing Room and charming Bar.
A luxurious location from which to
explore Northumbria. Colour brochure &
tariff (including Special Breaks) available
by telephoning:
(0434) 84-8888

a privately-owned and family-run site which has a reputation for its neatness and tidiness. There are extensive grassed areas alongside the beautiful river bank where many people bathe, paddle or scramble over the rocks (all at their own risk). A major attraction for adults and children alike is the miniature railway which is ¼-scale, 15 inch gauge, and pulls passenger carriages. The site also has light refreshments, water, and toilet facilities.

A site at Whistle Crag enables visitors to have a magnificent view of the dale looking across at Mickleton, Harter Fell, and Kirk Carrion. Here the river meanders about, very different from its course higher up the dale. There are no facilities for picnics, but there is the chance to have a picnic in the car, especially in the times of year which are not so warm, when there may still be a clear and interesting view. A second similar site is on the B6277 on the bank known as Folly Bank with Eggleston below. Here a whole panoramic view of the upper dale opens up before you.

Also included in this guide is the picnic site at Alston for the South Tynedale Railway. This is England's highest narrow gauge railway built on the site of the old Alston-Haltwhistle line. There is also an excellent cafe, and souvenir shop at the site. The railway goes as far as the Gilderdale halt but it is intended to continue it much further.

A short excursion from Teesdale is the journey into Weardale to see Killhope Wheel. This can be approached from Langdon Beck via St. John's Chapel, from Newbiggin, or from Middleton via Stanhope. Here is an excellent picnic area which can be used before examining the various processes involved in leadmining at the museum there and looking at the splendid wheel used for crushing the ore.

The Teesdale area is undoubtedly very rich in possible picnic sites and the locations described above offer planned developments for the visitor. As mentioned earlier, many visitors have their own preferences, though these are normally unplanned and 'unofficial' sites with few, if any, facilities. During the last summer many of these localities were very popular and several are briefly mentioned below.

The Weelhead Sike car park, located beside Cow Green Reservoir, is not a picnic site, and there is no room for games. Nevertheless it proves to be a popular choice with the visitors for such an outing. Here, the peace and natural beauty of the High Pennines can be enjoyed, and there are also the alternatives of closely following the adjacent Widdybank Fell Nature Trail and experiencing the power of the nearby Cauldron Snout Waterfall. There are toilet facilities available.

Further down the dale, at Middleton-in-Teesdale, can be found the picturesque and secluded area beside Beck Road on the east bank of the Hudeshope Beck. Though private land belonging to the Raby Estate, picnicking tends to be tolerated for the benefit of local people from the village.

At the western end of the road, along the northern side of Baldersdale, is a very small site with no facilities. Much visited in the summer, its attractions are the beautiful moorland scenery and the availability of a walk along the public footpath leading further up the dale.

At the mouth of this dale, in the village of Cotherstone, is another small site. Located beside the River Balder and below the armchair-shaped hollow known as The Hagg, it offers some seclusion yet it is not far from the facilities offered by the village.

If you wish to recommend any other locality, then please write and let us know.

Time to relax at Scoberry Bridge(MP)

Landforms to Visit

At the head of any list of landforms to visit would automatically be High Force, Cauldron Snout, Low Force and Ashgill Force. However this area affords a variety of other features, which, although not as spectacular, display much beauty and character and are well worth a visit. Included in my selection are several of the most important viewpoints. Please notice that not all of these localities are accessible to the public and if they are not clearly visible, you will need special permission for access from the land-owners. An ordnance survey map of the area will help you locate these landforms · map references are given for each selection. Please note that an admission charge may be payable at certain localities.

ABBEY GORGE (067148) Located 1 mile SE of Barnard Castle and crossed by the Abbey Bridge of 1773, this picturesque, wooded and steep-sided gorge is incised into the grey limestone known locally as 'Teesdale Marble'. Here the River Tees passes through a narrow channel between the stepped, horizontal layers of limestone. The deep, dark waters make the riverside 'Paradise Walk' (downstream from Abbey Bridge on the south bank) both peaceful and mysterious. A fine view is also gained from the lofty Abbey Bridge itself.

ASHGILL FORCE (757405) Located in youthful South Tynedale beside the B6277, 17 miles NW of Middleton-in-Teesdale and 4 miles SE of Alston. It is a 15 metre (50 ft) vertical fall in the valley of the Ash Gill Beck. Several public footpaths lead to the fall, both from the B6277 and from Garrigill and Crossgill (an O.S. map will be needed to locate these footpaths). Although the B6277 crosses the fall at the bridge at O.S. map reference 758405, a long walk will have to be undertaken to reach it. However the extremely deep, wooded ravine known as Ash Gill, and the succession of small falls leading up to Ashgill Force itself, certainly add to the grandeur of this natural attraction · especially when the beck is in spate.

BLEABECK FORCE (874279) Located beside the Pennine Way on the Blea Beck which flows into the River Tees from the S bank about 1000metres upstream from the mighty High Force. This is a small attractive fall which provides much appeal in times of above-average run-off. It is not a fall to make a special journey to see, but provides a pleasing attraction on a riverside stroll along the 874279 Pennine Way having crossed the River Tees by way of the bridge (map reference 889283) about 500 metres SE of the High Force Hotel.

CAULDRON SNOUT (814287) Located below Cow Green Reservoir and Dam about a 2 mile walk from the lakeside Weelhead Sike car park in Upper Teesdale. This is one of England's most beautiful and most powerful landforms and is in fact England's longest and largest cataract. A footpath does descend the 60 metres beside the 500 metre long stairway of eight boiling falls, to the snout of the cascade itself. A breath-taking spectacle but great care must be taken because the footpath is slippery, difficult and dangerous. Haunted by the 'Singing Lady'. No visit to Teesdale would be complete without experiencing the power and beauty of this natural attraction.

COW GREEN RESERVOIR (811310) Located about 3miles W of Langdon Beck. Though not a natural lake, this 2 miles long expanse of water, set against the background of the mighty Pennine Hills, provides a scene of great beauty. From the Weelhead Sike car park these views extend across the extensive uninhabited moorlands to the broad summit of Cross Fell, 893 metres (2930 ft) above sea-level.

CRONKLEY SCAR (840294) Located within the Upper Teesdale National Nature Reserve this 100 metre high, whinstone cliff, which attains a summit height of 547 metres (1794 ft), dominates the landscape of this part of the dale. There is no access to the scars of this Whin Sill outcrop but fine views are gained from the B6277 and the Hanging Shaw picnic area (867298).

FAIRY DELL (912262) Located at the edge of the dark, vertical, whinstone Holwick Scars to the S of the road to Holwick about 2 miles W of Middleton-in-Teesdale. In the past, also known as Fairy Glen, this picturesque hidden gorge and waterfall were a major tourist attraction. However the 300 metre walk through Mill Beck Wood and beside the Mill Beck itself, is on the private land of the Strathmore Estate and since there is no public right of way then permission for access must be obtained.

GIBSON'S CAVE (909288) Located on the Bowlees Beck a short walk from Bowlees Picnic Area and Visitor Centre, 3 miles NW of Middleton-in-Teesdale. The walk to the 'cave' is on the private land of the Raby Estate owners who have kindly granted permission for access. Here a small picturesque, 6-metre-drop waterfall, known as Summerhill Force, flows over a hard band of limestone. It must have been at the end of the ice-age when vast amounts of meltwater thundered over the fall

The imposing ruins of Brough Castle(JW)

The popular South Tynedale Railway(JW)

The pretty town of Appleby(JW)

Alston (JW)

that the underlying, softer shale was undercut to form the large overhang now known as Gibson's Cave.

HARTSIDE CROSS (647418) Located about 6 miles SW of Alston this magnificent viewpoint marks the summit of the Hartside Pass over the Pennine Hills via the A686. Here at 580 metres above sea level is one of the best viewpoints in England. At the top of the steep scarp marking the western edge of the Pennine Hills it is possible to look across the green Vale of Eden some 500 metres (1640 ft) below, to the mountains of the Lake District and the west coast of England. On the north-western border of the area covered in this book, it is some 30 mls (48km) by road from Middleton-in-Teesdale via the B6277, Alston and the A686.

HIGH CUP NICK (746263) Located on the Pennine Way long distance footpath about a 7 mile walk from the Weelhead Sike car park beside Cow Green Reservoir, and a 4 mile walk from the village of Dufton. However the journey to this breath-taking viewpoint and landform should not be undertaken unless you are fully equipped and experienced in walking on these wild Pennine Fells - and please remember that it is an uphill climb to the 'Nick' and a long return walk to your starting point. Also known as 'Eagle's Chair', having once been the haunt of the Golden Eagle, it overlooks a 200 metre (650 ft) deep ravine known as High Cup Gill. At the head of this typically U-shaped, glacial valley is a horse-shoe shaped outcrop of whin sill which forms spectacular cliffs and screes and adds to the overall grandeur of this magnificent landform and viewpoint over the contrasting low and level Eden Valley.

HIGH FORCE (881284) England's largest and most impressive waterfall, is Teesdale's best-known attraction. Like so many of the waterfalls and rugged scars which give Teesdale so much character, it owes its existence to the dark, fine-grained, crystalline igneous rock called dolerite and known locally as whinstone.

The 'Force' consists of two falls, one at either side of the huge central tower, but except in times of flood, only the southern fall operates. Flowing over the hard whinstone cap-rock, the river plunges 21 metres to the dark, deep plunge pool below where it erodes the 'softer' underlying layers of shale and limestone and undercuts the fall. This action has caused the waterfall to retreat and form a magnificent gorge.

In spate, the river, roaring over this fall, must have been an awesome sight. Local tradition has it that once in every fifty years or so, the river surges over the whole fall. However, since the completion of Cow Green Reservoir in 1970 the floodwaters have been controlled to some extent, and it may be that one will never again experience High Force in its past magnitude. But even today in times of exceptional rainfall and melting snow it still provides an awe-inspiring sight of uncontrollable fury as the roaring waters surge over both sides of the waterfall leaving little of the central column uncovered. It is also interesting to note that even before the reservoir was constructed, in the great floods of 1869, not all the fall was covered. It was at that time reported that an area of rock about the size of a sheep was still visible above the foaming waters.

The famous 'Tees Roll' is another feature of the river also less common and less severe since the regulation of floodwaters by the reservoir. This wave of flood water can sweep down the river without warning at any time of the year. Violent rainstorms on the high fells can bring danger to those enjoying finer weather along the lower parts of the river. On the 24th June, in the summer of 1880, one such 'roll' swept down the river and trapped two men on the central column, 24 metres above the pool below. One man was pulled to safety by means of a rope but sadly the second man, Mr. G.H. Stephenson of Gateshead, was swept away and drowned when, as he was being hauled through the water, his rope snapped.

These events serve as warning today because, beautiful and magnificent as High Force may be, it can also be very dangerous.

HOLWICK SCARS (9026) Overlooking the dispersed settlement of Holwick on the S bank of the River Tees about 3 miles NW of Middleton-in-Teesdale. Spectacular, vertical, whinstone outcrops which are impressive from both near and afar. At the north-western end of this dark, forboding cliff-line, a deep cleft isolates a large outcrop which is known locally as Holwick Castles. Once popular spot for rock-climbers, but on private land, and permission has been suspended by Strathmore Estate.

HORSESHOE FALLS (947268) Located in the valley of the Hudeshope Beck about half a mile N of Middleton-in-Teesdale. This is a miniature waterfall and gorge only about 3 metres high. Not a feature to make a special journey to see, but if one is in the locality it is in an attractive setting where the beck flows over a limestone cap rock which overlies a greater thickness of softer shale. On private land, it is visible from the narrow Beck Road which passes thhe very edge of both gorge and fall.

JACK SCAR CAVE AND GORGE (948277) Located in the valley of the Hudeshope Beck about 1 mile N of Middleton-in-Teesdale. A large and very dangerous, vertical-sided limestone gorge, cut by a waterfall long since disappeared. The limestone cliffs are unstable and large blocks of stone often fall into the gorge. This landform has been a popular feature with visitors for a very long time, as has Jack Scar Cave, whose small, hidden entrance has been used by many people in the past, though today, like the limestone cliffs above, it is in an equally dangerous state. It must be remembered that they are on private land and no access is available without prior permission of the landowner.

LOW FORCE (904280) Located on the River Tees, a short walk from Bowlees and the B6277 and 3 miles NW of Middleton-in-Teesdale. A very popular beauty spot where the river flows over an outcrop of whin sill and forms a series of picturesque falls. In the past this waterfall was also known as Little Force and Salmon Leap. A few metres downstream is the famous Wynch Bridge and the rocky whinstone gorge cut by the retreating waterfall.

MEETING OF THE WATERS (084145) Located 3 mile SE of Barnard Castle. Here at the confluence of the River Tees and River Greta is the small beauty spot made famous by the artists Cotman (1805) and Turner (1820) and the writer Sir Walter Scott (1812). The River Greta has cut a dark gorge into the limestone rock and this is crossed by the quaint Dairy Bridge, once the 'haunt' of the ghost, the 'Mortham Dobby'.

STAINMORE SUMMIT (901123) Located on the A66(T) only a few hundred metres within County Durham from its border with Cumbria. This is one of the few trans-Pennine routes. Here at the summit of the Stainmore Gap or Pass (447 metres) is a viewpoint over the wild, bleak, monotonous Pennine Moorland and the youthful River Greta which flows into the River Tees, E of Barnard Castle. A small roadside parking area, near to Rey Cross, will give you a chance to survey the lonely inhospitable landscape.

STANG FOREST (022076) Located near the watershed on the southern slopes of the Tees Basin. From the car park above the forest and from the short walk to Hope Scar (472m - 1550 ft) are excellent viewpoints, in fact some of the best in England. On a clear day it is possible not only to enjoy the panorama of Teesdale, but also that of the Stainmore Pass, the Pennine Hills and rural County Durham. It will also come as a surprise to see the lofty towers of Durham Cathedral and Penshaw Monument so far to the north, as well as the distant landmarks of urban County Cleveland and even ships in the North Sea waiting to enter the mouth of the River Tees.

TAN HILL (897067) Located on the watershed between the Tees Basin to the north and that of the River Swale to the south. Another viewpoint over the bleak Pennine Hills. On a clear day worth a visit to experience the lonely, unspoilt moorland environment and the open views. At 528 metres (1732 ft) above sea-level, the inn located on this site is reputed to be the highest in England.

TEESDALE CAVE (866311) Located in the scars of a limestone outcrop high on the valley side to the N of the River Tees and about 1 mile E of Langdon Beck. The walks from the Hanging Shaw Picnic Area and Langdon Beck lead to the foot of these scars and at an altitude of almost 500 metres (1640 ft) above sea-level offer excellent views over Teesdale. However the scars themselves are on private land and there is no public right of access. The Teesdale or Moking Hurth cave is a site of historical importance as by 1888, James Backhouse of York had excavated the cave and as well as finding the bones of lynx and wolves, uncovered the 3000 years old skeleton of an iron-age maiden who had made the cave her home. The entrance to the cave was superstitiously named Hobthrush Hole or Fairy Hole.

WHISTLE CRAG (977247) This is a popular viewpoint on the B6282 about 2 miles E of Middleton-in-Teesdale. A small, roadside layby offering an excellent panorama over part of Upper Teesdale from a high, exposed vantage point 200 ft (60 metres) above the river.

YAD MOSS (781358) Located on the B6277 between Middleton-in-Teesdale and Alston this viewpoint marks the boundary between County Durham and Cumbria and the watershed between the river basins on the Tees and South Tyne. On a clear day this spot provides clear views E and SE to Cross Fell (at 893 metres the highest Pennine peak), Little Dun Fell (842 metres) and capped by the masts of the Civil Aviation Authority Wireless Station, Great Dun Fell (847 metres). However the descent NW into South Tynedale and that SE into the valley of the Harwood Beck provide a whole range of attractive scenes of great variety.

The imposing ruins of Bernard's Castle(JW)

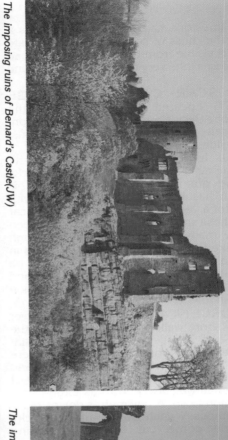

The marvellous setting of Raby Castle(JW)

The majestic grandeur of Bowes Museum(JW)

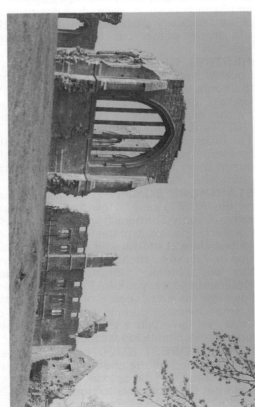

The impressive remains of Egglestone Abbey(JW)

One of the region's beautiful reservoirs(JW)

Whistle Crag's panoramic views (JW)

Beautiful banks of the River Tees(JW)

The rural splendour of Upper Teesdale(JW)

The Teesdale Area and its borders are extremely rich in places of historic interest. Therefore to help you enjoy your visit to the area, I have selected 26 sites of particular importance and appeal which are also an essential ingredient of the history and character of this magnificent region of England. Please note that some of these sites are not open to the public but are included because of their visual attractiveness and historic significance. For those which are open to the public an admission fee may be charged.

APPLEBY CASTLE

Appleby Castle is thought to have been built by Ranulf de Meschines as were Brough, Brougham and Pendragon. In 1157 Malcolm IV, King of Scotland, surrendered the castle along with his claims in Cumbria, to the powerful Henry II. Henry granted it to the Morville Family and it was Hugh de Morville who probably built its fine keep which is still intact. With the invasion of William the Lion in 1174 the castle was surrendered to him until his capture and imprisonment. It was then held by the Crown, the Viponts and finally the Cliffords. A wall tower is of the C13th but a considerable amount of building work was done by the Cliffords in the C15th. John Clifford built the gatehouse in 1478 and the hall, chapel and great chamber were built by Thomas, Lord Clifford, in 1454, who was later killed at the battle of St. Albans. Like many other Cumbrian and Yorkshire strongholds, it was restored by Lady Anne Clifford (in 1651) who made it her home, and her son-in-law rebuilt the east wing.

The building is now the headquarters of Ferguson Industrial Holdings and is used as an administrative centre, but the keep is now open to the public · and the hall sometimes. The original moat of the castle and the grounds have been converted to house endangered species · farm animals, as well as wildfowl and also large birds can be observed here.

BERNARD'S CASTLE

Located at Barnard Castle and sited at the Scar Top overlooking the Tees from the north bank, the first castle was probably founded by Guy de Baliol about 1100, but his nephew, Bernard, was largely responsible for the construction of the stone enceinte and it is after him that both the castle and town are named. The castle covers a large area (2.9 hectares) and is composed of four wards. The outer ward, which contained the main entrance, once behind the present King's Head Hotel, is now a field used by a local farmer. In the Middle Ages it contained the chapel and stables and was a refuge for the townspeople during time of invasion. The Middle Ward was through the Constable Tower, sometimes known as the Many Gates Tower because of its system of multiple gates. Here were the smithy and a brewhouse and bakehouse. From here one could cross a drawbridge either into the town ward or the inner ward. The town ward included a large open area, but also granges, a malt kiln, and the famous Brackenbury Tower, named after Sir Robert Brackenbury, Richard III's lieutenant of the Tower of London, who originally came from Sellaby (now the home of Lord Barnard!) and who was at the Tower during the disappearance of the Princes. The inner ward was the most fortified area including the chief lodging (in the Mortham Tower), the Lord's Chamber with Richard III's bristly boar on the soffit of its perpendicular window, the Great Hall, and the prison. But its most imposing structure is the Round Tower (see under Barnard Castle).

Famous owners of the castle and of Teesdale include John de Baliol, founder of Baliol College, Antony Bek, the most powerful Bishop of Durham ever (in military not spiritual terms); the fabulous Guy de Beauchamp, Earl of Warwick; Warwick the Kingmaker, Richard III and Sir Henry Vane the Younger. The castle was besieged in 1216 and probably again in 1265; strongly fortified against the Scots at the beginning of the C14th; surrendered to tenant rebels during the Pilgrimage of Grace 1536; its last siege was in 1569 (see under Barnard Castle). Fine views of the castle can be seen from Startforth, and from the Round Tower lovely views up the river.

BLAGRAVE'S HOUSE

Located on The Bank in Barnard Castle, this is one of the oldest buildings in the area. Named after the Blagrave family who were once innkeepers here. The present building dates from the early C16th though the foundations, cellars and 'secret passageway' are even earlier in origin. Sadly its appearance is not as authentic as a few years ago because recent restoration work led to most of the four-storey projecting bay having to be replaced. It is said that Oliver Cromwell rested here when he visited Barnard Castle on October 24th 1648. Another tale tells of the land and house being granted by King Richard III to Joan Forest · the widow of Miles Forest who may have disposed of the two princes in the tower for this king. After a variety of uses, entry is now normally only available to those using the restaurant facilities.

BOWES CASTLE

Located in the Bowes village 4 miles south-west of Barnard Castle and to the north of the River Greta, it consists of a three storey rectangular keep and very little else, and this is quite rare. The keep was built between 1171 and 1187 by Richard the Engineer for King Henry II because the duke of Britanny had died without male heirs. A subsequent Duke of Britanny, who had married into the family, got the castle back into his hands in 1233. In the C15th it was owned by the Fitzhughs, now a much more important family than when they first hunted around Cotherstone! The castle was sited right in the Old Roman fort of Lavatrae. What other buildings there were is open to question. The castle was besieged in 1173 by William the Lion but he had to abandon it in the face of a large army from England led by the archbishop of York! The Constable of Barnard Castle, Henry Fitzhugh, besieged and took over the castle for a time in 1322 while the duke of Britanny was in Parliament!

BOWES MUSEUM (Featured elsewhere)

BOWLEES VISITOR CENTRE

Located in the hamlet of Bowlees about 3miles
north-west of Middleton-in-Teesdale, it is based in one of the many chapels of the dale. This former Primitive Methodist Chapel built in 1868 now has a very different function. Developed by the Durham County Conservation Trust, its exhibition displays the life and history of the dale as well as geology and natural history. Open to the public.

BROUGH CASTLE

Located in the Eden Valley on the outskirts of Brough and on the western edge of the Pennine Hills. Built on the site of the Roman fort of Verterae, which guarded the western end of the Roman road across the Pennines via the Stainmore Gap.

It was begun before the end of the C11th as there is still some early Norman herring-bone masonry. It was in royal hands in 1174 when besieged by William the Lion and the Scots. They captured the outer palisade, then besieged the tower and burnt it. The present keep was rebuilt after this time, probably by Henry II. The Round Tower, Clifford's Tower, was built about 1300 by the first Lord Clifford who descended from the Viponts who held it before them. The hall block was built by later Cliffords. In 1521 the castle was accidentally set alight, but Lady Anne Clifford restored it between 1659-62. It was not to last however. Her son-in-law stripped it to repair Appleby in 1695, and in 1763 its stones were used to repair Brough Mill. Considering its destruction it is surprising how much remains. Fine views can be obtained from the top of the keep.

COLDBERRY MINE

Located in the valley of the Hudeshope Beck about 2miles north of Middleton-in-Teesdale. Here can be seen an old mine-shop, mine entrance, spoil heaps and the huge 'Coldberry Hush', a V-shaped gash on the hillside above. At its peak this mine produced large amounts of lead ore for local smelt mills. This is an excellent example of the extractive operations of the lead-mining period of the C18th and C19th. A public footpath leads to this mining site and an inspection of an O.S. map will indicate where you are allowed to go. This is private land and the old workings are highly dangerous.

DOTHEBOYS HALL

Located at the western end of Bowes village 3miles south-west of Barnard Castle. This was the Academy of schoolmaster William Shaw and was visited by Charles Dickens on February 2nd, 1838. The Academy and Shaw are reputed to be the Dotheboys Hall and Wackford Squeers of Dickens' novel 'Nicholas Nickleby'. It is not an impressive building but did provide an interesting part of the character of the dale. A private dwelling, not open to the public, but clearly visible beside the A66(T).

EGGLESTON HALL

Located on the north bank of the River Tees beside the old Eggleston Bridge and on the edge of Eggleston Village. The first mention of the village came at the end of the C12th and in subsequent centuries a hall or Manor existed here. In 1663 Christopher Sanderson was reported to have been the Lord of the Manor but it was whilst this position was held by one William Hutchinson, that the present hall was constructed about 1813. In the grounds are the ruins of the largely C18th church. Today the hall is owned by Lady Gray and is used as a Finishing School for girls. A fine view of the hall is gained from the south bank of the river. Not open to the public.

EGGLESTONE ABBEY

Located beside the Thorsgill Beck on the south bank of the River Tees half a mile south-east of Barnard Castle. Founded by Ralph de Multon in 1195, it survived until 1540 and the 'Dissolution of the Monasteries'. This was the abbey of the Premonstransion Order of monks, known locally as the "White Canons" because of their white robes. An impressive vista is that gained from the hilltop viewpoint

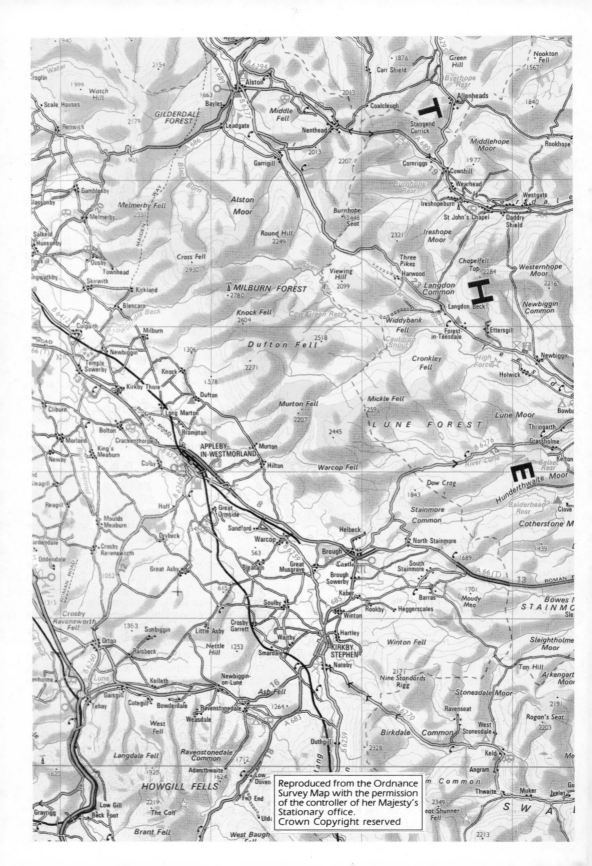

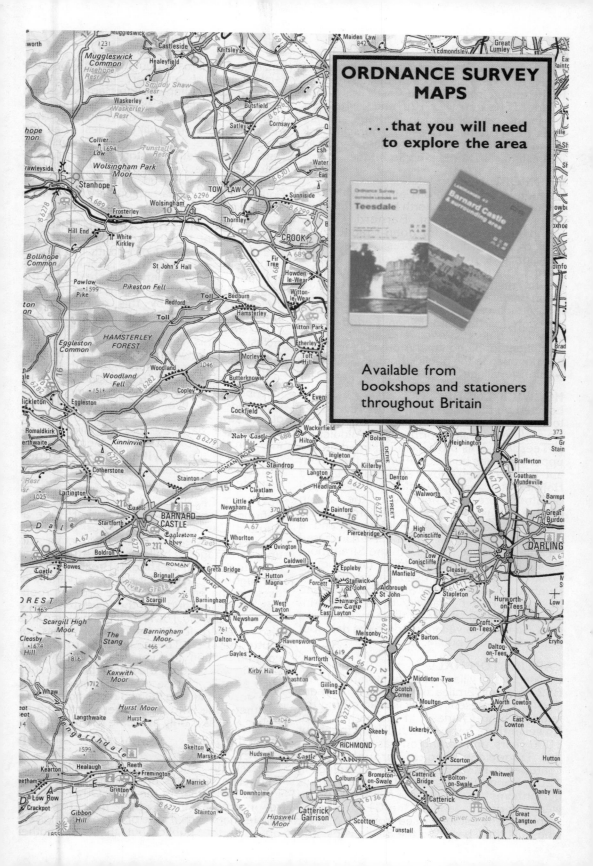

overlooking the abbey from the north bank of the River Tees. This is located beside the road to the abbey from Barnard Castle via Abbey Bridge. The extensive C12th and C14th ruins are in the care of English Heritage and are open to the public. The tiny Thorsgill Beck which flows beside the Abbey is crossed by an interesting C17th pack-horse bridge.

GAINFORD HALL

Located in the village of Gainford which sits astride the A67 on the north bank of the River Tees 7miles east of Barnard Castle. Completed in 1605 for John Cradock, the vicar of Gainford, this impressive Jacobean mansion is a major feature of this historic village. Though in a ruinous condition in the C19th, restoration work has been able to retain nearly all of its original structure. Within its grounds can be seen the C17th circular dovecote of the Elizabethan Period which provided pigeon's eggs and the essential ingredient for pigeon pie! A private residence and not open to the public, though visible from within the village.

HOLWICK LODGE

Located on the south bank of the River Tees to the west of the dispersed settlement of Holwick and 3miles northwest of Middleton-in-Teesdale. This prominent landmark in the upper dale was built at the end of the C19th and has also been known as Holwick Hall and Holwick Mansion. Now belonging to the Earl of Strathmore, the nephew of the Queen Mother, it was initially built for Cosmo Bonsor who was a Member of Parliament and a director of the Bank of England. He had leased an area of grouse moor from the Strathmore Estate and the lodge was to be his 'shooting box'. The sandstone used came from the Dunhouse Quarries near Staindrop, having to be transported by railway to Middleton-in-Teesdale station, and from there by horse and cart. An impressive landmark in the dale, but not open to the public.

LARTINGTON HALL

Located in the village of Lartington beside the B6277 about 2miles north-west of Barnard Castle. The present Hall was built during the reign of King Charles I in the early C17th. However there has been a hall here for about 1000 years, and Lartington was mentioned in the Doomsday Book. Throughout the centuries it had many owners including, in 1208, Robert de Lascelles, then the Marquis of Northampton and later the Maire family who were the descendants of the C12th Lord of Appleby. The estate passed from the Maires, who built the Chapel, to the Silver Tops, and

finallt the Withams although all were variously related to one another. Henry Witham founded the Witham Hall in Barnard Castle, and built the ballroom as a geology museum. His successor, the well known priest Monsignor Witham, built the priest's hall and grand entrance. After a period of misuse the Hall is now being restored as a private residence. It is not open to the public but visible from the road and, during the Teesdale Country Fair, from Lartington Park itself which surrounds the house.

LONG MEG AND HER DAUGHTERS

Located about 12miles south-west of Alston and 7miles north-east of Penrith this almost 4000 years old stone circle is ranked fourth in importance in England. Reached from the small village of Little Salkeld it is just beyond the area covered by this guide, but its importance, as well as its position at the foot of the steeply rising Pennine Hills, warrants its inclusion. This circle of 64 stones has a diameter of between 93 and 110 metres. Long Meg, a pillar of red sandstone, the largest of all the stones, is located outside the circle. Inscribed upon it, is a rather strange cup mark surrounded by two concentric circles. Two other stones located outside the circle represent a 'gateway' into the circle. Local tradition has it that Long Meg and her daughters were witches who turned themselves into stone. On private land but restricted access is available.

MARKET CROSS

A famous landmark in the Market Place at Barnard Castle. Not a cross as the name suggests - instead a highly distinctive and unusual octagonal building. Constructed and given to the town by Thomas Breaks in 1747. Throughout its history it has had a variety of uses. In the early 1800's the upstairs room was used as a court and the lower room as a jail. Once the old Town Hall, the building was also referred to as the 'Butter Cross' or 'Buttermarket'. These latter terms were common when the veranda encircling the building was used for the sale of farm produce such as milk, cheese and, of course, butter. The story explaining the two bullet holes in the weather vane is told elsewhere in the book. Public access is only available to the veranda.

MIDDLETON HOUSE AND CLOCKTOWER

Located in Middleton-in-Teesdale these distinctive buildings are a monument to the industrial heritage of the Dale. Other features of interest include the 'new town' of Masterman Place. None of these buildings are open to the public, but these and other features in the village, such as the Victorian-style drinking fountain, stand as testimony to past eras in the Dale's history. Further details about this industrial heritage can be found elsewhere.

MORTHAM TOWER
Located on the east bank of the River Greta only a short distance to the south of the River Tees and 2 miles south-east of Barnard Castle. The Pele Tower or fortified farmhouse was built in the early C15th by a Lord of Rokeby when his home was destroyed during a Scottish raid. Some later additions were made at the end of the C16th. Today it is a private residence and not open to the public though it is clearly visible from the public footpath that passes the side of the building.

NEWBIGGIN CHAPEL
Not a very old building, but the oldest Methodist Chapel in continuous use in the world. It was begun in 1759, opened in 1760, and extended in 1860. At present the building is being renovated but keys can be obtained from the Post Office. Wesley probably preached here a number of times.

PARKER'S KILNS
Located in the valley of the Hudeshope Beck about half a mile north of Middleton-in-Teesdale. Lime kilns were once an essential part of the farming landscape because lime was burnt and spread onto the soil to neutralize the acidity caused by the abundant rainfall. Sadly, nearly all of these largely C19th kilns have disappeared as a result of lime now used by farmers for walls and other buildings. These kilns, however, are still in a relatively good condition. The original kiln, the most northerly of the four seen today, was first operated and possibly built by my great,great, great grandfather, Thomas Parker, and his family. Limestone was obtained from the Skears Quarry above the kilns and the fuel, initially obtained locally, was transported by horse and cart from Middleton Railway Station. The kilns are an important reminder of our industrial heritage. Visible from the road but on private land so access not allowed without the permission of the Raby Estate.

PIERCEBRIDGE ROMAN FORT
Located beneath the village of Piercebridge on the north bank of the River Tees about 10miles east of Barnard Castle. Built to protect the river crossing and the Roman road known as Dere Street. The first fortifications here probably date from about 125 AD and the reign of the Emperor Hadrian. However the present excavations have revealed later defences of about 270 AD and these covered a 5 hectare site upon which the present village developed. Detailed excavations commenced in 1933 and are now almost completed. Many excellent relics have been uncovered. Though of historic importance, the excavated area does not offer an imposing appearance.

RABY CASTLE (Featured elsewhere)

RAVENSWORTH CASTLE
Located in the rural village of Ravensworth some 8 miles south east of Barnard Castle, just beyond the borders of the Tees Basin. This C12th Norman castle, visited by King John in 1201, is reputed to have been built upon earlier defensive works of an even earlier age. It is thought to have been an early stronghold of the mighty Fitzhugh family, and, in fact, it was Henry Fitzhugh who, in 1397, obtained permission to enclose as a Park some 80 hectares of land surrounding the castle. Today it has lost much of its past grandeur having been largely dismantled in the early C16th. The masonry was used as building-stone in the construction of the village and the surrounding farms with the local bailiff being reported to have removed vast quantities for his own use. Clearly visible but not open to the public.

REY CROSS
Located to the south of the A66(T) about 6 miles east of Brough and west of Bowes near the summit of Stainmore Pass. This ancient monument was erected by King Edmund of Northumbria (who died in 946) to mark the boundary between his English Kingdom of Northumbria and the Scottish Kingdom of Strathclyde. It was here that Eric Bloodaxe, the last Viking King, was killed in battle in 945 so marking the end of Viking rule in Northern England. Until 1092 it remained as the boundary of England and Scotland. At this time William Rufus of 'Richmondshire' seized all the land as far as Carlisle. However as late as 1258 this monument was described by the Bishop of Glasgow as being the southern boundary of his diocese! It has also been referred to as Rere, Rer and Rei Cross which has been interpreted in several ways including 'cairn', and 'royal cross'. All that remains of this former wheel-headed cross is its shaft, and the inscriptions and carvings, once reputed to have adorned both sides, have long since weathered away. Not an impressive monument but of great antiquity.

The extensive wooded greens of Staindrop village(JW)

The elegant Lartington Hall(JW)

The emblem of Teesdale - the famous Blue Gentian(JW)

The clocktower at Middleton-in-Teesdale(JW)

The ancient Eggleston Bridge over the Tees (JW)

The foreboding cliffs of Cronkley Scar(JW)

Low Force - a famous beauty spot(JW)

The wooded gorge approaching High Force(JW)

ROKEBY HALL

Located on the south bank of the River Tees near its confluence with the River Greta. A fine building, once the home of the Rokeby family but as a result of Colonel Rokeby being on the losing side of the Royalists in the Civil War, he was forced to sell his estates to the Robinson family. It was later purchased by the Morritt Family in 1769 and has remained in their possession as a private residence to this day. It was here in 1809, 1812 and 1813 that Sir Walter Scott stayed whilst writing his romantic novel 'Rokeby'. There is a fine walk along the edge of Rokeby Park which leads to the famous 'Meeting of the Waters', not far from Scott's cave. The house still remains in the Morritt family today but now the house and park are open to the public at various times in the week. The house was the home from 1805-1905 of the famous painting the 'Rokeby Venus' by Velasquez but has still a unique collection of needlework pictures done by Anne Morritt who lived from 1726 to 1797.

ROMALDKIRK CHURCH

Beautiful church dedicated to a strange saint who declared he was a christian the moment he was born, preached a sermon, then died three days later. But there is some doubt whether this is the St Romald referred to. Decorated chancel with piscina (for washing communion plate) and perpendicular tower. Effigy of Hugh Fitzhenry one of the Fitzhughs of Ravensworth, and Cotherstone.

STAINDROP CHURCH

Fine old church including Anglo-Saxon nave with original windows built into the walls, and much work of all medieval periods from that time. Round transitional arches in the main body of the church (or nave); Early English north transept with pointed (lancet) windows. Two storey north-east vestry from which the priest looked through the squints. Chantry Chapels created in the south aisle in 1343. Only surviving rood screen in the country. Alabaster and wood effigies of the Neville family.

STANWICK FORTIFICATIONS

Located between the villages of Forcett and Aldborough St. John about 4 miles south east of Winston. These extensive earthwork fortifications that cover a 344 hectare (850 acre) site were constructed by the Brigantes tribe who ruled the north of England. Under the leadership of their King, Venutius, they prepared to meet the Roman advance. When the Romans arrived in England, the Brigantes were ruled by Queen Cartimandua. She made peace with the Romans but on two occasions her people revolted against the Romans - the second time, under the leadership of her husband, Venutius. On each occasion the Romans helped to overthrow the rebellions. However the proud Brigantes overthrew their Queen and once again followed Venutius against the Romans. Sadly, as a result of the reputed treachery of Cartimandua, the Romans, under Agricola, defeated Venutius in a battle around AD70 and destroyed the strength of resistance against them. Part of the fortifications are in the care of the Department of the Environment and are open to the public.

WALWORTH CASTLE

Located between the villages of Heighington and Piercebridge, a few miles to the north-west of Darlington. It is one of the last border fortifications built towards the end of Queen Elizabeth's reign at the end of the C16th. Sited near the 'lost' Saxon village of Walworth, which has long since disappeared, it fortunately escaped damage in the Border or Civil Wars. The fine 3-storey building, with semi-circular angled tower, once played host to King James VI of Scotland whilst he was on his way south for his Coronation as King of England. Today it welcomes more guests because it has recently opened as a restaurant.

WYNCH BRIDGE

Located about 200 metres south-west of the hamlet of Bowlees and the B6277 this small, suspension footbridge may not seem to be of historic importance. However the present bridge dates from about 1830 and the earlier bridge it replaced was believed to have been the earliest suspension bridge in Europe. It was built in 1704 by lead-miners from Holwick who needed to cross the River Tees to get to the Pikelow and Redgrove Mines located on the fells above Newbiggin.

This first bridge consisted of two 18 metre long chains attached to rocks on both banks of the river. Planks were laid on these and one hand-rail attached to the eastern side. In 1771 the great floods damaged the bridge but it was to be repaired. Tragedy came in 1802 when eleven people were crossing the bridge and one of the main chains broke, with surprisingly only one person being drowned. It can be reached by the public footpath from Bowlees and is a popular beauty spot.

The Life of a Dalesman

The Teesdale area today is still basically a farming area though a small amount of quarrying and the last remains of a once flourishing lead and barytes mining industry still continue. However, times have been hard and change has come slowly to the people of the dales. Reg Wearmouth, a good friend and former neighbour of mine, witnessed these changes and had many interesting recollections of life in the dale.

Born on September 18th, 1900, in the small whitewashed stone-built No.1 Thompson Cottages, Forest-in-Teesdale, Reg grew up in difficult times. His father was a lead miner who worked at Nenthead near Alston. On a Monday morning with his 'wallet' holding his week's food on his back he would set off to walk the 14 mile (22km) journey arriving after several hours in time to start work at l pm, his shift finishing at 10 pm that night. He would then lodge in a mine shop and work long hours on Tuesday, Wednesday and Thursday before setting off to walk home after work on Friday afternoon with his £1 weekly wages in his pocket.

When Reg left Forest-in-Teesdale school at 14 he also took a job at the mines - this time at Cow Green Barytes mine, now submerged beneath the waters of Cow Green Reservoir. He would leave home at 5.30 am and walk the 5 mile (8km) journey, arriving in time to start work at the washing rake by 7 am. Work finished at 5 pm and he would then walk his 1½ hour journey home, having earned one shilling and three pence for that day's work. In winter the long and arduous journey to work still had to be made, despite freezing temperatures, blizzards and drifts.

Two years later he took a job as farm lad for Thomas Gibson at Widdybank Farm. However, Mr. Gibson soon vacated the farm and Reg had to take another farm job with Mr. Carr of Bunker's Hill, Garrigill, near Alston, just before he was called to Carlisle for his army medical in 1918. Fortunately, though he was passed fully-fit, the First World War ended and Reg returned to Teesdale where he worked at Park End Whinstone Quarry at Holwick for 4½ years.

Reg's family had moved from Thompson Cottages when he was about 12 years old. They moved to Chapel Cottage, only about 100 metres from their previous home. Now they were moving again to Underhuth, a mile up the dale at Langdon Beck. About this time Reg commenced work for the council, helping to lay the 'tarmac' road from Yad Moss to Harwood. He later found employment at Bradley Quarry (just opposite Thompson Cottages) where he worked for another couple of years.

It was now 1933 and Reg moved with his parents to a farm at Ettersgill less than a mile from his birthplace. Sadly, his father died within the year and Reg took over the farm which was to be his home until 1975. In 1938 he married Winnie and together they worked hard on this small hill farm. It was then 21½ hectares (53 acres), of which 11 hectares were meadow, and this supported 15 dairy cattle, 60 sheep and 30 hens. In their early farming days the milk was made into butter on the farm and every market day they would take the bus to Barnard Castle to sell their butter and eggs at the Buttermarket which can be found in the market place. Other farm income was raised from the sale of some cattle and sheep at the Darlington and Barnard Castle Livestock Marts, and from the wool which was collected and taken to the West Riding of Yorkshire textile area. It was not until later that milk was collected and taken to Appleby.

Times were especially difficult in the winter of 1947 when they were 'snowed-in' for two months and lost half of their sheep. Work was also hard as everything was done by hand or by horse-drawn equipment. In fact it was 1954 when they purchased their first tractor.

In the years leading up to Reg and Winnie leaving the farm one of their two sons, Carl, became a partner in the farm. In fact today Carl runs the farm along with his wife Dorothy who was 'Shepherdess of the Year' in 1973. Their other son, Alwyn, found employment in the dale when the dams and reservoirs such as that at Cow Green were being built. After their completion he had to leave the dale to find employment elsewhere.

In 1975 Reg returned to No.1 Thompson Cottages, the house where he was born. Nine years later in 1984, he moved to Alston Road, Middleton, where he died in 1985. His wife, Winnie, is still living there. Reg was well loved in the dale and will be long remembered. He used to say without hesitation that, despite all the advancements and improvements that the world can boast of, they were 'happier times' when he was young. They had to make their 'own enjoyment' as Reg told me and 'it wasn't uncommon to find a houseful of friends and neighbours on an evening'. Having read about his life you may find this a little hard to believe, but the friendly and helpful nature of the dalesfolk was forged in these hard times.

Summerhill Force and Gibson's Cave(JW)

High Force - England's largest waterfall(JW)

Barnard Castle's Market Cross(JW)

The famous Wynch Bridge(JW)

Raby Castle

Raby Castle, the seat of Lord Barnard, is undoubtedly one of the finest and most interesting castles in all of the country. The earliest record of the castle is in thereign of King Canute who, in 1017, not only ruled over England but also Norway and Denmark. Styling himself as the 'Emperor of the North', he ruled his kingdom from his mansion at Staindrop. There are several pieces of evidence for this belief. As well as it being recorded that King Canute gave his Manor of Staindrop to Saint Cuthbert in 1030, there are several notable Danish connections in the area. The name of Staindrop was derived from 'Stenderup' which was Danish for stone village, and the name Raby comes from two Danish words which mean village and secluded corner. It is also believed that the lower portion of Bulmer's Tower, which is of Danish style and origin, was in fact King Canute's mansion. The only difficulty with this is that Canute's mansion was said to be at Staindrop, not Raby, and the dating of the base of the tower has long been questioned. But it is strange that high up on this tower are two 'b's said to refer to Bertram de Bulmer, who was related to Isabella de Neville, which may suggest an early date for this tower.

In 1131 the castle fell into the hands of Dolphin, a Saxon noble and the son of Uchtred, the Earl of Northumberland. He was succeeded by his son Meldred and he, in turn, by his son Geoffrey FitzMeldred who assumed his mother's name of Neville. (The Nevilles were descendants of Gilbert de Neville who was Admiral of William the Conqueror's fleet when he invaded England in 1066). It was later, in 1379, that most of the present castle was built by John de Neville. It stayed in the possession of the family until 1569 when it was forfeited, along with their lands, to the Crown as a consequence of the treachery of Charles Neville, the sixth Earl of Westmorland, who helped plan the 'Rising of the North' in the Baron's Hall. It remained a Crown possession for 43 years until the estate, which included both Raby and Barnard Castles, was purchased for £20,000 by Sir Henry Vane whose grandson, Christopher, became the first Lord Barnard.

Today, Raby Castle is a major tourist attraction. Within its ancient walls there is much of interest to enjoy, for not only is it fully furnished in mainly Victorian style but there are also the medieval kitchens and servant's quarters, a fine collection of carriages and other horse-drawn vehicles, and of course, the extensive gardens. However, perhaps the most remarkable feature is the beauty and character of the castle itself. Set in English parkland its herds of red and fallow deer complete a picture of grace, tranquility and strength which has probably changed little for over six hundred years.

Raby, like so many other castles, has a rich store of legends. Ghosts and secret passages are the centre of rumour and speculation wherever you may be, and here it is no different. It is said that there is a secret underground passageway which leads from the castle to Staindrop Church over one mile distant - though it is now reputed to be blocked off. But more interesting are the ghosts of Raby - not just one but three!

Perhaps the best-known tale is about Elizabeth, the first Lady Barnard. She and her husband Christopher, the first Lord Barnard, were greatly displeased at their eldest son Gilbert's marriage to Mary Randyll. In fact Elizabeth, 'Old Hell Cat' as she was called, was so angry and obsessed with Gilbert's disobedience that along with her husband she decided to strip and despoil the castle that her son was to inherit. The lead was stripped from the roof, glass removed from windows, doors taken out, floors pulled up, furniture sold, trees felled in the park and even the herds of deer killed - but before Raby Castle itself could be destroyed court action by their son enforced Lord and Lady Barnard to cease the destruction and to restore the building at the then tremendous cost of £3000. However, this action was too late to prevent everlasting damage for as a result of 'Old Hell Cat's' sale of the contents, little if any of the original furniture and relics of the Nevilles now remain.

At night, and even through the day, Elizabeth is said to haunt the castle in an uncontrollable rage and knitting with red-hot knitting needles, whilst during the evening, as the sun sets, the golden-red glare of these needles can sometimes be seen flashing from the battlements as 'Old Hell Cat' inspects her castle before nightfall.

If you catch a glimpse of her then don't linger, for to meet 'Old Hell Cat' with her centuries of hate and fury is said to be worse than meeting the devil himself. Oh! - and for those among you who are not so nervous, don't despair if you miss her for you may be 'fortunate' enough to meet either the exiled Charles Neville, the 6th Earl of Westmorland who may be visiting from his lonely grave in Holland or instead the headless body of Henry Vane the Younger!

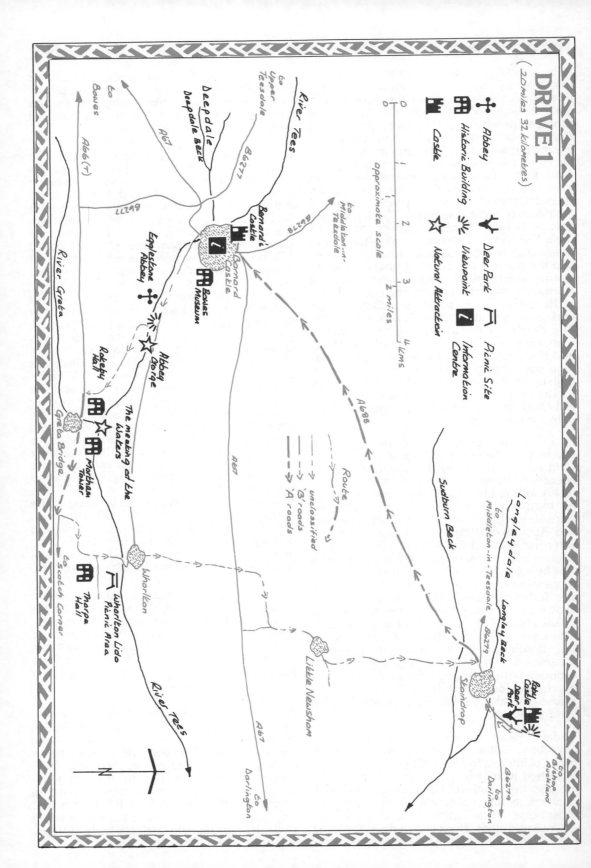

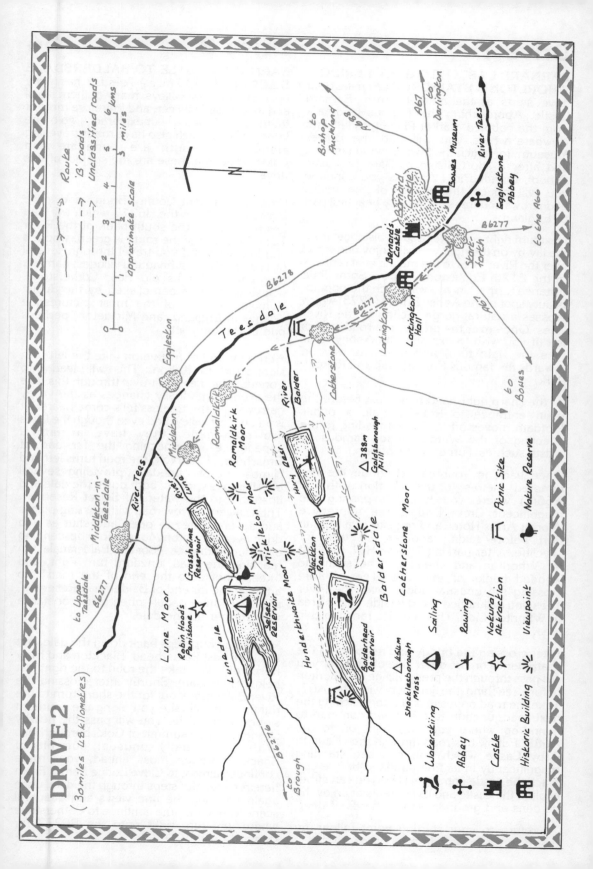

Drive 1

BARNARD CASTLE TO GRETA BRIDGE, WHORLTON & STAINDROP (20 miles) Our drive starts at the Market Cross, Barnard Castle. Approaching this famous landmark from the cobbled Market Place turn left into Newgate where you will find the Bowes Museum, for which the town is world famous, and after a short distance, Barnard Castle School, founded in 1883. As you continue you will notice the beauty of the fields, hedgerows and trees of this very beautiful part of England.

Next turn right and, after a short distance, from the lay-by on the right you will enjoy fine views over the River Tees to the magnificent remains of the C12th Egglestone Abbey. Some little distance further on you will reach the popular beauty spot of the Abbey Bridge (1773) which crosses a natural gorge section of the River Tees. Once over the bridge, the road swings left (if you wish to examine the Abbey ruins take the right turn) and winds its way on towards the famous Rokeby Hall and Rokeby Park.

At the sharp right-hand bend, just before the main entrance to Rokeby Hall, a public footpath moves off to the left leading to the 'Meeting of the Waters', made famous by artists such as Turner and Cotman.

Once back in your car, continue the few hundred metres to the junction with the A66(T) where you turn left passing the magnificent Greta Bridge, the impressive 'Morritt Arms Hotel' and the site of a Roman Fort before taking another left turn for Wycliffe. After passing Thorpe Hall, turn left for Whorlton and ahead can be seen the wooded banks of the River Tees. Before crossing the unusual bridge over the River Tees you will notice the riverside picnic area of Whorlton Lido. This is a nice family picnic area.

After crossing the bridge and negotiating the sharp bends on the other side of the river you will pass through the pretty village of Whorlton before reaching the junction with the A67. Take the road opposite and after reaching the next road junction turn left and continue to Staindrop where you turn right on to the A688. Follow this road through the village to Raby Castle which you can see standing magnificently in its fine parkland before you reach the castle entrance. Here you can either explore the castle and its contents or enjoy the gardens and grounds with its herds of deer.

To return to your starting point follow the A688 through Staindrop to Barnard Castle.

Drive 2

BARNARD CASTLE TO BALDERSDALE & LUNEDALE (30 miles) Teesdale has many beautiful tributary valleys, many of them small and inaccessible by car, and therefore most of them remain relatively unexplored. Two of the larger valleys which also have roads travelling along their length are Lunedale and Baldersdale and these are the subject of this drive.

Cross the ancient County Bridge and leave Barnard Castle on the B6277 which will lead upstream along the south bank of the River Tees. This part of the route is green, wooded and low-lying and you travel through several of Teesdale's most beautiful villages, namely: Lartington, with its old Hall; Cotherstone, whose castle was demolished by the Scots; Romaldkirk, one of the most picturesque villages in England; and Mickleton, perhaps one of the longest!

At the far end of Mickleton take the left turn signposted to Kelton. This will lead into Lunedale, and as you travel through this dale the scenery gradually changes as the valley narrows and the treeless fells come nearer. It is an unspoilt valley, and even though the lakes are man-made, they have a natural appearance. Approaching the far end of Grassholme Reservoir, the road turns left and climbs out of Lunedale, providing several excellent viewpoints, both down the dale and upstream to the waters of Selset Reservoir. This is a very narrow road with passing-places and several gates to open and shut as you drive over Mickleton Moor before descending over Hunderthwaite Moor into Baldersdale. On reaching the road junction, turn right, and "keep right onto the end of the road", to arrive at the far end of Balderhead Reservoir, at a spot where people often picnic or start a walk further up the dale.

Retracing your steps back down the dale, but this time past Balderhead, Blackton and Hury Reservoirs, you take the road to the right just below Hury Dam. Shortly after crossing the River Balder look out for the sharp turn to the right which will take you along the southern slopes of the dale. You will pass the nearby strange-shaped summit of Goldsborough Hill. With the equally unusual summit of Shacklesborough Moss ahead, your route continues almost to Clove Lodge Farm . From here retrace your steps through the dale, once again enjoying the fine views and beautiful scenery, but this time continue to Cotherstone where you turn right onto the B6277 for Barnard Castle.

UPPER TEESDALE AND WEARDALE (47 miles) Leave Middleton on the B6277 in a NW direction. There are fine views to the south over the river and farming landscape to Holwick Fell and the high cliffs of the disused Park End Quarry, Holwick Scars and the rock outcrop known as Holwick Castle. There is also the noble Holwick Lodge where several Royal visitors have been entertained.

At Newbiggin-in-Teesdale you will find a good example of how rural depopulation and improved communication have destroyed old village structure. In the last century it was served by a shoe-maker, grocer, draper, tailor and blacksmith but these have sadly disappeared under the shadows of progress.

At the hamlet of Bowlees there is not only the Bowlees Picnic Area and footpath to Gibson's Cave and Summerhill Force Waterfall, but also the Bowlees Visitors' Centre. Nearby are the beautiful waterfalls known as Low Force and the historic Wynch Bridge, and these are easily reached by a short pleasant walk.

On approaching the High Force Waterfall Car Park and Picnic Area, one must beware of walkers on the verge-less roadside, as they make their way back from the river.

Further along at Forest-in-Teesdale, is the small Hanging Shaw picnic area, also a fine viewpoint. Facing this spot is the dark rugged whinstone outcrop of Cronkley Scar. After periods of rainfall silvery waterfalls pour over its near vertical cliff from Cronkley Fell above. White Force is that pretty waterfall seen on the left.

Continuing, notice the grey limestone scars high above the road to the right. This is the site of the famous Teesdale Cave known also as Moking Hurth or Backhouse Cave.

The former entrance, now blocked by a limekiln, was known as Hobthrush Hole or Fairy Hole and led to a fine cavern system. Entering by another access, Mr.James Backhouse of York carefully examined it in 1878 and eventually found not only the bones of over 30 animals, including the now-extinct wolf and lynx, but also the skeleton of an ancient human cave-dweller, possibly an Iron Age maiden.

After crossing the Langdon Beck there are the winter ski-slopes to the right and fine views over the Harwood Beck to the left. The settlement known as Harwood is the collection of all these white-washed stone cottages strung out along the length of this valley.

It is also possible to see the River Tees shining in the distance as it nestles between Cronkley Scar and Widdy Bank with the slopes of Mickle Fell behind it.

From this road we should be able to see the three peaks of Great Dun Fell, Little Dun Fell and Cross Fell on the skyline. If you find a suitable place to stop there are also fine views back down the valley of Harwood Beck to Cronkley Scar and the Tees Valley itself.

Soon you will pass from County Durham into the County of Cumbria at Yad Moss (590 metres -1935ft), which derives its name from "a yard of moss", and if you look at this bare treeless moorland then the exposed edges of the peat hags show a great thickness of peat often largely consisting of moss.

The site offers fine views of several Pennine summits. Meldon Hill (767 metres) looks much higher than the distant flat-topped Cross Fell, at 893 metres (2930ft), the highest peak in the whole of the Pennines. On its slopes the River Tees is born.

Over the watershed between the river basins of the Tees and the South Tyne, you can see the youthful River South Tyne in its picturesque valley as it flows on to Alston, the highest market town in England.

Leave Alston on the A689. This will take you through Nenthead and over the watershed into the valley of that third great northern river, the Wear.

Keep on the A689 past the famous Killhope Wheel and through Ireshopeburn and St. John's Chapel until you reach Daddry Shield.

Here, turn right opposite the telephone box and continue for about half a mile to where you take another, but very much smaller road to the right.

This climbs out of Weardale into Teesdale along narrow, unfenced, passing-place roads. Several gates have to be opened on this raod but it is well worth it because of the beauty of the area.

Descending there are magnificent views over the 'patchwork-quilt' fields of Upper Teesdale. On arriving in Newbiggin-in-Teesdale, take the first road to the right and on meeting the junction with the B6277, turn left for your destination.

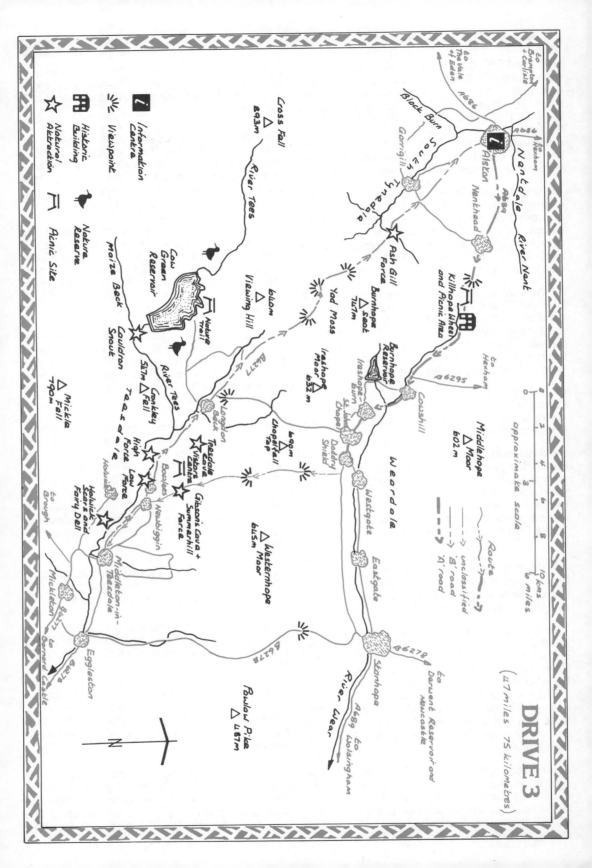

DRIVE 3

(47 miles 75 kilometres)

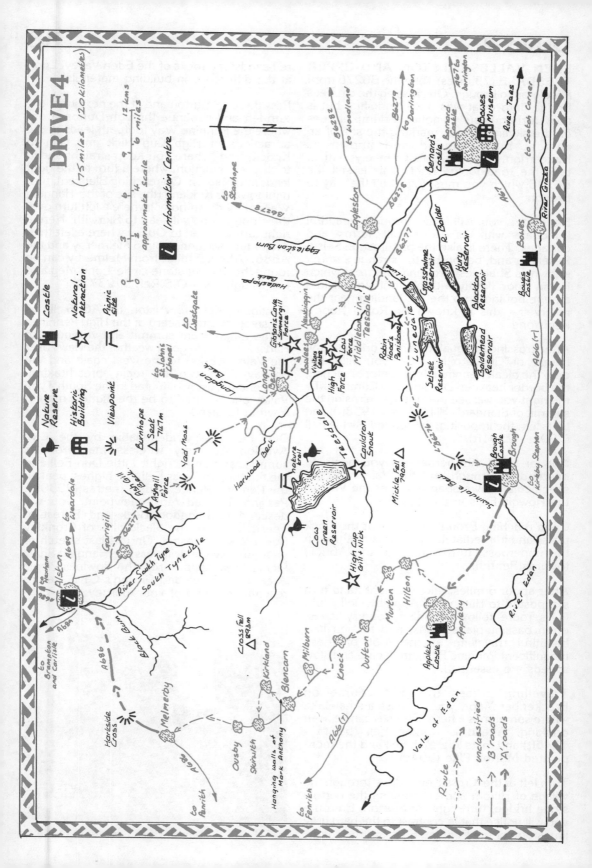

Drive 4

EDEN VALLEY, ALSTON AND UPPER TEESDALE (75 miles) Take the B6276 from Middleton to Brough. On crossing the old Tees Bridge (into what was once Yorkshire but is now Durham) you will notice a clump of trees on the skyline ahead, marking the site of an ancient burial mound and known as Kirkcarrion. After about half a mile you must take the road to the right. This is still the B6276 which you must follow all the way to Brough.

En route, you will pass through beautiful Lunedale with its stone-built farms and cottages. There is also the picturesque Selset Reservoir and, beyond it, the strange summit known as Shacklesborough Moss from which Robin Hood 'let fly with his foot' and kicked a huge boulder into the air, landing near the reservoir - this is known as 'Robin Hood's Penistone'.

After crossing the quaint, narrow bridge at the hamlet of 'Grains o'th' Beck', you will climb onto the bleak Pennine Moors before reaching the border between Durham and Cumbria. To the right you will see the strange cairns on the summit of Standards Hill (597m - 1958ft), and to its left, the imposing, flat-topped Mickle Fell (790m - 2591ft).

Not far from this border, as you begin to descend to Brough and the Vale of Eden, spectacular views open out over the Vale to the Howgill Fells in the distance.

Upon reaching Brough, turn left at the clock tower and immediately upon passing through the underpass, turn right onto the A66(T) towards Penrith.

After about 6 miles, take the right hand turn signposted to Hilton and Appleby Golf Club. (This route follows winding country lanes, often passing-place roads, and though it is beautiful travelling at the foot of these magnificent Pennine Hills, great care and slow speeds are essential).

Travelling across the golf course on Brackenber Moor, you will pass a small lake where sometimes a herd of horses can be seen drinking. Ahead is Roman Fell (593m - 1945ft) and to its left, Mell Fell and the more pointed Murton Pike (594m).

Turn left at the 'Cross Keys', drive through the village of Hilton, and on crossing the narrow stone bridge, turn right for Murton. En route you will notice that in contrast to the hard grey limestone of the Pennine Hills, are the softer, red-sandstone rocks of the Eden Valley. Look at the difference in building materials!

Pass through Murton and at the next junction, turn left and continue through Dufton (from where the Pennine Way footpath leads to the attractions of High Cup Nick and Gill) to Knock, from where you keep straight ahead to the next junction, where a turn to the right leads into Milburn. On reaching Blencarn, turn right towards Kirkland (the site of the 'Hanging Walls of Mark Anthony') where a left turn over the stone bridge will lead to Skirwith. Here a right turn will lead to Ousby where a left then a right turn will bring you to Melmerby and the A686. (About 5 miles from Melmerby can be found the ancient stone circle 'Long Meg and her Daughters' - O.S.Ref. 572372).

Continuing right, for Alston, the A686 climbs the steep, western scarp of the High Pennines to the magnificent summit and viewpoint of Hartside Cross. In good weather the views over the Vale of Eden to the west coast and the Solway Firth can be really breathtaking. Descend to Alston, situated in the South Tyne Valley and reputed to be the highest market town in England.

Dun Fell, easily identifiable by the Civil Aviation Authority wireless masts on its summit, and on its right, Little Dun Fell and the flat-topped Cross Fell, the highest peak in the Pennine Range at 893 metres (2930ft). Passing the Yad Moss viewpoint, you will descend to Langdon Beck and Forest-in-Teesdale where the black cliffs of Cronkley Scar are so imposing. On this last stretch of your journey you will pass the Hanging Shaw Picnic Area, High Force, the Bowlees Picnic Area, Low Force and Gibson's Cave, before reaching the end of your journey.

Brough Castle's impressive ruins(MP)

Walk 1

SELSET RESERVOIR (1¼)

Start and Finish Point: O.S. Grid Reference 918216

Selset Reservoir is managed by the Tees Division of the Northumbrian Water Authority. It is as a result of their courtesy that there are several sporting activities undertaken here such as sailing, fishing, birdwatching and walking.

The walk I have selected is simple and short. The Northumbrian Water Authority are willing to allow you to walk at liberty through the reservoir grounds or along its banks, but there are several rules to observe and certain dangers to consider.

Selset Reservoir was built in 1960 in the valley of the River Lune, a tributary of the River Tees, and serves the purpose of both regulating the flow of water down the River Lune into the River Tees and providing a domestic water supply.

Access to the reservoir is found to the left of the B6276, about four miles from Middleton-in-Teesdale. The start of the selected walk is from the car park on the north side of the reservoir and simply follows the roadway across the dam and back.

Don't be misled by the distance; from the car park to the other side of the dam is about 1000 metres and if you stop to admire the remarkable beauty of the surrounding views as you cross the dam and to study the sailing, fishing or wild-life, then your return trip may take at least one hour.

As you leave the car park and approach the dam you will cross a bridge under which is the overflow channel for the waters to drain off when the reservoir is full. It is only now that you will begin to realise the scale of the operations and the planning that has gone into the construction of this most magnificent dam and reservoir.

Continuing, you should begin to experience and enjoy the clean country air and the peace and tranquility of the countryside. Surrounding you is some of the highest enclosed farmland in England. Here are the dry-stone-wall enclosed fields pushing up towards that beautiful, yet hostile, purple-brown moorland.

Most of the land here only affords rough grazing for sheep (mainly black-faced Swaledales) though a few cattle may be seen on the better pastures. As the winters in this area are very severe the best land is used as hay meadows to grow winter fodder for the animals.

Progressing across the dam the views across this narrow valley broaden as you look north-eastwards to where the waters of the River Lune twist their way lazily through the five arches of the stone-built Grassholme Bridge towards the picturesque Grassholme Reservoir in the distance.

Beyond Grassholme Reservoir you can see the Northern slopes of the Tees Valley which look so beautiful in the sunlight.

In the foreground between Grassholme Bridge and Selset Dam is a Wild-Life Sanctuary into which entry is forbidden. However, with binoculars, you may be fortunate enough to pick out some of the numerous birds or animals which are found in the reservoir area in general.

The animals include the mole, rabbit, hare, fox and stoat, but there is a much larger list of birds and a pocket book of birds would help identification.

From the dam, if you look westward over the peat-stained, brown waters of Selset Reservoir, there is much to see; there are the boats of 'Selset Sailing Club' putting out on to the reservoir; whilst along the banks you may be fortunate enough to see the fishermen making their catch.

In the distance, beyond the waters of the 2 miles long Selset Reservoir, is a beautiful landscape where the River Lune and its tributaries make their way towards you between wooded banks; and behind them, to the right, are the slopes of the area known as Lune Forest leading up towards Mickle Fell 2591ft (790 metres) and to the left the slopes of Stainmore Common.

When you reach the end of the walk at the far end of the dam and look westward, you are looking at 2 miles of tree planting along the reservoir's southern shore. Its main purpose is to provide a visual amenity with the secondary advantage of providing a commercial crop of timber at the turn of the century. Work began in 1973 with the ploughing, draining and clearing of the land preceding the planting of a wide variety of trees and shrubs approaching 110,000 in number!

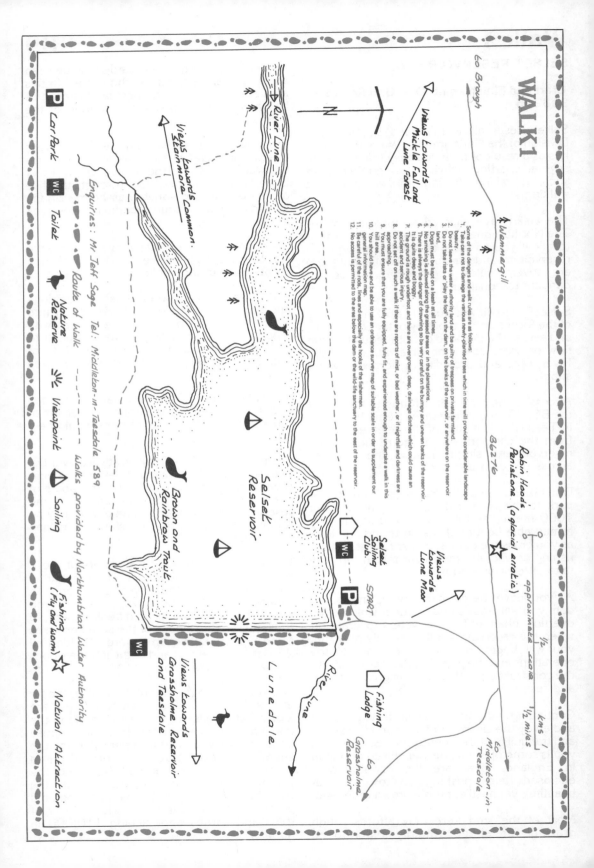

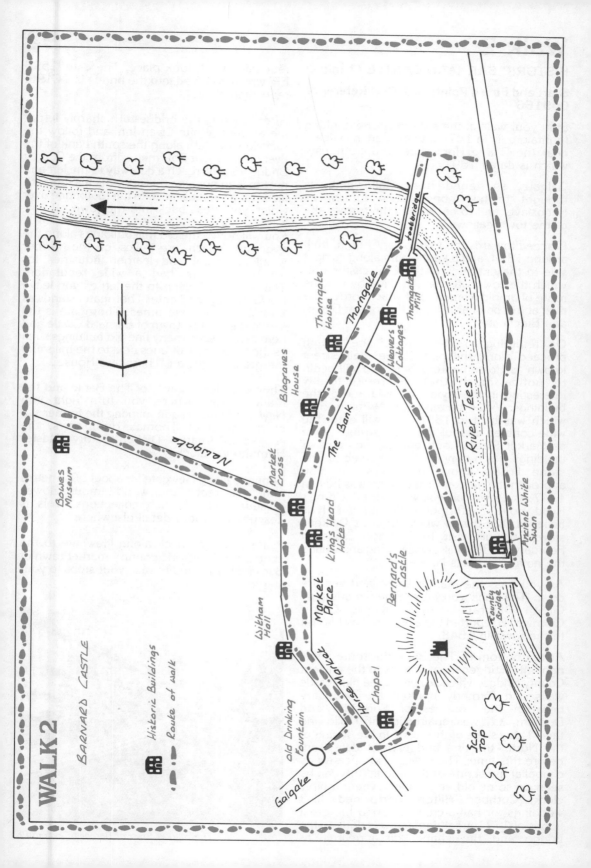

Walk 2

HISTORIC BARNARD CASTLE (2 miles)

Start and Finish Point: O.S. Grid Reference 049166

Start your walk at the old sandstone drinking fountain built in 1874 and located in Galgate near the 'Three Horseshoes' public house, which is dated 1691.

Galgate, shortened from Gallowgate, is thought to have once been known as Hangslave, and to have been the former site of the town gallows.

Proceed towards the Methodist Church, built around 1894, and take the path along its right side to the entrance of the C12 castle after which the town was named. Nearby lies the route of an old Roman road which forded the river at this point as it linked the forts at Bowes and Binchester.

On returning to the front of the church proceed along the part of the main street known as Horsemarket where you will begin to notice much that is architecturally interesting in the style, size and age of the buildings. After passing the Witham Hall, which was built in 1854, you will enter the wide cobbled area of the main street known as Market Place. Look out for the dates of buildings which may be found carved on the stone lintels above doorways. As you approach the Market Cross which was built in 1747, as a town hall, you will notice the 'King's Head Hotel', a former coaching inn. It is believed that this is where Charles Dickens stayed on his visit to Barnard Castle in February, 1838, whilst researching and writing the novel 'Nicholas Nickleby'.

As you pass the Market Cross and venture down 'The Bank' you will see the famous early C16th Blagraves House where Oliver Cromwell is reported to have rested on his visit to the town in 1648.

At the bottom of The Bank the route veers right into Bridgegate and leads to the ancient County Bridge, which lies below the high castle walls and formerly marked the boundary between the counties of Yorkshire and Durham. As it was repaired in 1569 following the 11-day siege of the castle in the 'Rising of the North' the first bridge must date from before this time. There was also once a tiny chapel at the centre of the bridge (this can be seen on some old engravings) where a bible clerk, Cuthbert Hilton, performed illicit weddings for half-a-crown. During the great floods of 1771 great damage was done to the bridge and the chapel disappeared as

rebuilding work took place. The date '1596 ER' which is carved into the bridge is a C19th rebuilding error.

After crossing the bridge turn sharply left at the ancient 'White Swan Inn' and follow the roadside footpath along the south bank of the river. After about 350 metres from the County Bridge you will reach a gateway to the left and next to it an opening through which a footpath leads for a short distance to the footbridge over which you cross back into the town.

You will notice the old mill buildings along the riverbank which are relics of the former woollen, carpet and leather industries for which the town had a wide reputation. Thorngate Mill, seen to the left as you leave the footbridge and enter Thorngate, stands as a reminder of these times. Thorngate is the site of the earliest town of Barnard Castle and here can be seen many fine old buildings such as the Weavers' Cottages next to the mills and the grand Georgian 'Thorngate House'.

Thorngate leads back to 'The Bank' and the Market Cross where you turn right into Newgate at the plaque marking the former site of the shop of Thomas Humphreys, the subject of Charles Dicken's story 'Master Humphrey's Clock'.

Continue along Newgate for about 500 metres until you reach the world-famous Bowes Museum with its rich collections. This is described in more detail elsewhere.

Make your way back along Newgate to the centre of this historic country market town of Barnard Castle and retrace your steps to your starting point.

The market town of Barnard Castle(MP)

Walk 3

A SHORT HILL WALK FROM MIDDLETON-IN-TEESDALE (2 miles)

Start and Finish Point: O.S. Grid Reference 947254

The walk itself commences in the centre of Middleton-in-Teesdale. Follow the B6277 south towards the River Tees. When you reach the Tees Bridge there is much to see. The bridge itself, at 700ft (213 metres) above mean sea-level, is a single-arch stone bridge built in 1811 upon the site of an earlier bridge which fell down soon after its completion. In previous times of flood the river has actually flowed through the upper pair of 'tunnels'. (These tunnels have now been filled in during strengthening work to the bridge).

You continue past the Auction Mart and take the sharp turn to the right along the minor road to Holwick. Almost immediately you must pass through the gateway to the left which leads from the road and on to farmland. Here the really hard work begins. Keeping close to the dry-stone wall on your left, follow the well-marked track up the slope towards the clump of trees known as Kirkcarrion. The slope is very steep in parts, but there are long stretches which afford much easier going. After about 400 metres you will reach a dry-stone wall field boundary. After passing through the gate, take a rest and enjoy the view. Middleton-in-Teesdale nestles below in the valley bottom. To the west can be seen the high cliffs of Holwick Scars and the patch-work quilt fields of the valley floor with its tree-lined river banks.

After about another 300 metres you will meet a fenced field boundary. Pass through the gate, closing it after you, and if necessary, take another 'breather', you will find the views are more impressive from here. You can look west towards Holwick 'Castle' and Holwick Lodge, north to the beautiful wooded valley of the Hudeshope Beck with Monk's Moor to its right, and east to the River Tees as it flows below the very steep slopes of 'Whistle Crag'.

After this well-earned rest there are only about 400 metres remaining of your uphill climb. Here you will reach another gate which marks the end of your journey (343 metres - 1125ft). About 300 metres beyond can be seen the trees of Kirkcarrion, the site of an ancient Bronze-Age burial mound. The views here certainly are impressive and make the tiring climb well worthwhile.

Walk 4

CAULDRON SNOUT AND UPPER TEESDALE NATIONAL NATURE RESERVE (8 miles)

Start and Finish Point: O.S. Grid Reference 853312

This walk is very rich in individual features of great interest which have been described in much detail elsewhere in this book. As this is a circular walk, it is possible to tackle it in either direction and from two major starting points. Perhaps the most popular would be Weelhead Sike Car Park beside Cow Green Reservoir, but I have chosen that starting point which does not result in a steep climb at the end of the walk.

Starting at the 'Langdon Beck Hotel', follow the minor road all the way to 'Cow Green Reservoir'. This 3 mile stretch of the walk steadily climbs over 130 metres (417ft) to the start of the Widdybank Fell Nature Trail, part of the internationally-famous Upper Teesdale National Nature Reserve. Trail guides are normally available from a dispenser in the nearby Weelhead Sike Car Park.

Follow the narrow tarmac road (which is the nature trail) to Cow Green Dam, below which is found the powerful Cauldron Snout waterfall, the largest cascade in the country. Great care is needed in following the precarious 'footpath' to the valley floor below.

At the foot of Cauldron Snout, turn left and follow the well-defined, though rocky, Pennine Way footpath. This leads below the dark, foreboding, whinstone cliffs of Falcon Clints, before reaching easier going on the level, grass banks of the widening valley as we approach Widdybank Farm. Continue on through the farmyard and leave the Pennine Way by following the rough farm track. This leads back to the road not far from your starting point, and although the public footpath does not follow this track all the way to the road, the farmer would prefer that all walkers use it to prevent damage to his pastureland, which is largely within the nature reserve. On reaching the road, turn right to complete the short distance back to your car.

This is a long and tiring walk over difficult terrain in part - so please be properly prepared. However, the beautiful views and unspoilt scenery of this part of Upper Teesdale, as well as the importance of the features that you pass, makes this one of the most rewarding routes in the area.

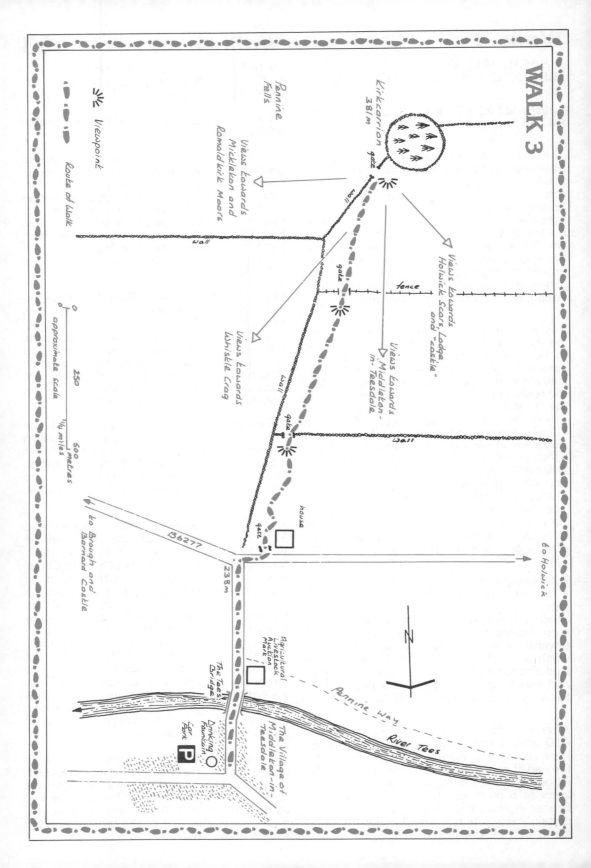

WALK 3

Kirkcarrion
381m

gate

Pennine
Falls

Views towards
Mickleton and
Romaldkirk Moors

Views towards
Holwick Scars, Lodge
and "castle"

Views towards
Middleton-
in-Teesdale

Views towards
Whistle Crag

wall

gate

wall

gate

fence

Wall

wall

gate

house

gate

to Brough and
Barnard Castle

B6277

238m

to Holwick

The Tees
Bridge

Agricultural
Livestock
Auction
Mart

Pennine Way

The Village of
Middleton-in-Teesdale

River Tees

N

Car
Park

Drinking
Fountain

P

Viewpoint

Route of Walk

0   250   500
         metres

0   ¼ miles
approximate scale

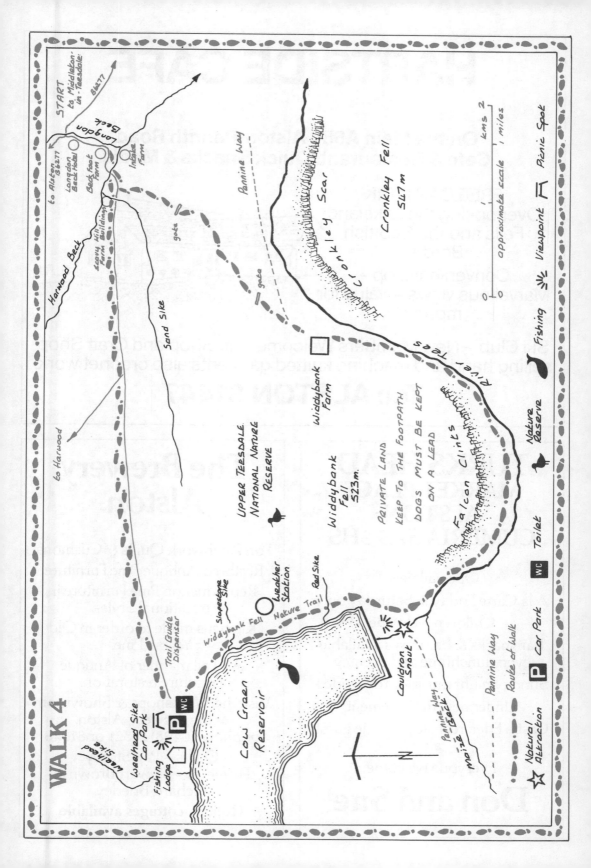

Alston

As well as having much to offer in itself and in the immediate vicinity, Alston is well placed as a centre for touring.

Carlisle, Hexham, Penrith and Barnard Castle are within twenty to thirty miles of the town, and all the area covered in this book can be conveniently reached from Alston.

The Lake District is upwards of thirty miles away with Ullswater the nearest lake. The Eden Valley is just a short drive away. Hadrian's Wall and its numerous Roman sites lie twenty miles to the north. Gretna Green and the Scottish Border are thirty miles away.

Alston, the highest Market Town in England, is in the heart of the North Pennines, in an eastern projection of Cumbria, near the borders with both Northumberland and Durham.

Although the town lies in the sheltered Valley of the River South Tyne, it is surrounded by the highest fells of the Pennine chain, which give birth to the rivers of the South Tyne, Wear and Tees. Alston is relatively isolated, and as a result has remained almost completely unspoiled. Old photographs in local shops show the town in the last century looking much as it does today.

The lower end of the town centre is called 'Townfoot', where the Town Hall, built in 1857 for £3,000, is situated. Further up the main street is 'Church Gaytes', built in 1681. Above the Parish church is the Market Cross. Down to the left is the oldest surviving part of Alston, known as "The Butts", a reminder of the need in Elizabethan times for men to practice archery. Up the main road to the right you pass the Old Quaker Meeting House, now the Toc H Headquarters; and the former Grammar School, dated 1828 and now the Fire Station. The top end of the town is known as the "Town Head".

In Alston there is now a new attraction - the narrow gauge South Tynedale Railway, the highest in England. There are refreshment and picnic facilities at Alston Station, as well as souvenir shop.

There is evidence of occupation of the Alston area in the Middle or late Bronze Age. At a later date a 'camp' was established at Hall Hill on the west bank of the South Tyne near its confluence with the Nent. The Romans constructed the north-south road known as the 'Maiden Way' and built the fort now called Whitley Castle, two miles north of Alston.

This impressive fort has a massive rampart and ditches, although it has been little excavated. It was built, probably in the C2nd, but modifications were made a century later as dedication slabs show. Alston itself may mean Alden's farm, but evidence of Saxon settlement is hard to come by. The medieval church of Alston was appropriated by Hexham Abbey, but it was demolished and rebuilt in 1769. This structure was itself demolished, and the present building raised in 1869-70.

It is important to see the Gossipgate Gallery which can be approached from the Butts. This displays art and craft work from the area, all under gas light which provides atmosphere to its exhibits.

The Alston Grammar School probably dated from the reign of Queen Elizabeth, although Appleby and Barnard Castle had grammar schools before the Reformation.

But the most important aspect of the history of Alston to consider is its leadmines. Leadmining is known here from very early on in the medieval period. In fact it is likely that the major development of the town occurred because of their presence. Originally it was the silver mines which attracted attention. The burgesses of Carlisle paid Henry I £5 for the old rent for the silver mine, and it is clear from later documents that the mine of Carlisle means the mine of Alston although the accounts to the sheriff went through Carlisle. The silver was used for coinage in the royal mint. Hugh de Baliol, lord of Barnard Castle, a little later tried to obstruct the miners who often crossed his own land in Upper Teesdale, but in 1235 they were taken under royal protection. Another landlord claimed that the miners were cutting down wood near their mines, for their own uses, and not for work in the mines. But the Alston miners became independent and self governing and their prosperity seemed assured. But towards the end of the Middle Ages, with a lack of fuel, the exhaustion of some seams, and competition, the mines were threatened. The Radcliffes took the mines over and it was said at the time that James Radcliffe, the Jacobite Earl of Derwentwater, could have raised a private army from his willing miners in the cause of 'The Old Pretender'. On his forfeiture, the mines were leased to the London Lead Company who developed model homes like Dufton and Nent Head, just as they did in Teesdale. (For more about leadmining - see the Leadmining section.

The early C19th was the heyday of Alston as a

mining town but by the end of the century lead mining had lost its significance. Now agriculture is to the fore.

Alston's Market Cross(JW)

Not far from Alston are a number of picturesque and interesting villages sited in the green valley of the River South Tyne.

Garrigill · the names means "Gerard's Valley" · is an attractive village four miles south of Alston up the South Tyne Valley. The 50 foot drop of the Ashgill Force is close by, and the Pennine Way passes through here.

Travelling north along the A689, you come first to Slaggyford (the name simply means a muddy ford), and then Knarsdale (the valley of the rugged rock). Knarsdale is a straggle of a village which boasts a C17th Hall, a Church and a Town Green. It lies between the A689 and the River South Tyne.

A gravestone in the churchyard at Knarsdale commemorates Robert Baxter, a shepherd, who died on the 4th October 1796, after eating a piece of bread and butter he found while climbing the fell to count his sheep. He died convinced that he had been deliberately poisoned by a neighbour after a violent quarrel, as this inscription on his tombstone shows:

"All you that please these lines to read,
It will cause a tender heart to bleed;
I murdered was upon the fell,
And by the man I know full well;
By bread and butter which he'd laid,
I being harmless, was betrayed.
I hope he will rewarded be;
That laid the poison there for me".

At Lambley a minor road off the A689 will take you to Greenhead and Haltwhistle. It was at Lambley that a convent of Benedictine Nuns was burnt to the ground by the Scots in 1296. Nearby is the famous Lambley railway viaduct which crosses the River South Tyne at a height of 110 feet, a monument to the railway age. The Haltwhistle to Alston line was completed in 1852.

Alston is a natural centre nestling in the beautiful South Tyne Valley below the wild unspoilt fells and peaks of the High Pennines. It is diffuclt to convey the attractions of Alston in words. The steep, cobbled streets, the stone houses and buildings, and the general unchanging air of the place give you a feeling of timelessness. But for the modern dress of the people, you would imagine yourself to have gone back in time a hundred years. Look at the old photographs you see in some of the local shops; the town looks much as it did then when the pictures were taken.

The South Tynedale Railway(JW)

Alston can offer all the amenities a visitor would expect in a small market town, indeed more. There are hotels, cafes, shops. pubs. Yet all around there is wild, almost untouched country.

The Romans passed this way and created the Maiden Way, their western route to Hadrian's Wall, and Whitley Castle, a huge fort north of Alston. Now instead of heavily armed legions, bands of peaceful walkers pass along the Pennine Way. If you do see "Roman" soldiers, you might not be dreaming · enthusiasts have recreated the scene.

HARBUT LAW

ALSTON, CUMBRIA CA9 3BD
Telephone: 0498 81447

Harbut Law is run by the Shepherd family and is ideally situated for touring the Lake District, Teesdale, Hadrian's Wall, Kielder Water and the Scottish Borders, also right on the Pennine Way.

Bed & Breakfast, evening meal optional.
Packed lunch available. Separate T.V. lounge.
Some rooms hot & cold. Separate bathroom.
Ample car parking facilities.

THE BLUE BELL INN

TOWNFOOT, ALSTON,
CUMBRIA CA9 3RN
Tel: (0498) 81566

The Blue Bell Inn is a listed building and dates back to the 17th century, with many original beams remaining.

All bedrooms have tea and coffee making facilities and washbasins.

The delightful restaurant is open throughout the day, with an excellent and interesting menu.

**REAL ALE, BAR SNACKS,
ACCOMMODATION, MORNING COFFEE,
SNACKS, AFTERNOON TEA,
LUNCHTIME AND EVENING MEALS**

Famous People

Many important and famous people have lived in or visited Teesdale over the years. Perhaps the most important inhabitants and visitors to the area have been the Kings of England and Scotland. It was possibly as early as 1017 AD that the famous King Canute, who ruled over England, Norway and Denmark, had a residence at the site of the present Raby Castle. In fact, according to local tradition, the lower portion of Bulmer's Tower, which possibly dates from Danish times, is reputed to be King Canute's royal residence and the small village of Staindrop the 'capital' of his realm. Raby Castle has other historical links with royalty as it was visited by Charles I, James I and Edward VII. It is also said that King John visited Bowes Castle and Ravensworth Castle and that King Edward stayed at Scargill Castle in 1323. Another castle, Bernard Baliol's castle, the English home of the Baliol family, gave rise to the growth of the town of Barnard Castle. In fact one of his descendants, Hugh Baliol, received King John at the castle in 1216. The Baliol family continued their importance in the area through Hugh's son, John Baliol, who not only became Regent of Scotland but also, along with his wife Devorguilla, was the founder of Baliol College at Oxford University. In 1292 their son, also called John, was crowned King of Scotland at Scone.

Visitors to Barnard Castle include the Lord Edward, later Edward I in 1268, and a colourful warrior Bishop of Durham, Bishop Bek, who owned the castle from 1296-1306 and is said to have done major repairs there. After the Baliols had been attainted as rebels, Edward I gave it to another important family, the Beauchamps - the Earls of Warwick. It is often said that they never visited the castle, but this claim is exaggerated. Guy de Beauchamp was also a legendary warrior as were his successors Thomas and Richard. The castle descended to Richard Neville, Earl of Warwick, known as the 'King Maker', who died in the Wars of the Roses. Edward II stayed in the castle in 1322, and Edward III a little later. Edward IV may have stayed in the Hospital of St. John the Baptist on Newgate.

In the C15th the castle was also the home of the Duke of Gloucester until he became King Richard III of England. A later visitor to Barnard Castle who also had associations with the Crown of England, was Oliver Cromwell, who rested here on October 28th, 1648.

The link with the Crown is still strong today, not only because members of our present Royal Family are occasional visitors to the area but also because Queen Elizabeth the Queen Mother and therefore Queen Elizabeth II and her children and grandchildren are direct descendants of the Bowes and the Strathmnore families who have lived in Teesdale for centuries. In fact one of their ancestors, Sir George Bowes of Streatlam, defended Barnard Castle for Queen Elizabeth I in the 'Rising of the North' in 1569.

Arising from local legend, perhaps two of the most surprising names linked to the area are Robin Hood and Cock Robin. You might well ask what they have to do with the Teesdale area of the High Pennines - so if you are sitting comfortably I will begin!

Once upon a time when Robin Hood, the outlaw, was possibly having a 'working holiday' in the area he provided us with a memento of his visit - Robin Hood's Penistone. This is a huge sandstone boulder with a circumference of about 13 metres and a height of about 2 metres. It is found perched on limestone bed-rock about 3 miles west of Middleton-in-Teesdale on the right of the B6276 Brough road after the entrance to Selset Reservoir. Geologists try to convince us that this rock is an erratic left by the Stainmore Glacier, but we believe the local tale which states Robin Hood, possibly upset at meeting no rich 'tourists', kicked the boulder from the summit of the 454m Shacklesborough Moss which lies 3 miles to the south of its present resting place.

The other Robin - Cock Robin, the subject of a children's fable, was born about 1840 at Ouler Hill, near the banks of the River Tees and not far from Barnard Castle. From here he made his first flight of about 7 miles to the village of Staindrop.

This beautiful area has been a source of inspiration for poets and artists alike. John Sell Cotman painted the well-known water colour of the beautiful Greta Bridge in 1805, and the famous Joseph Mallard William Turner shortly afterwards completed many drawings of the area, including 'The Meeting of the Waters', 'Barnard Castle', 'Egglestone Abbey' and 'High Force'. Poets too, have been inspired by this most beautiful part of England, including William Wordsworth, Sir Walter Scott, the local Darlington poet Horsley, and our own Teesdale poet, Richard Watson. Of these Sir Walter Scott and Richard Watson are the most prominent.

Sir Walter Scott was a friend of John Morritt who was the owner of the Rokeby Hall to which the famous work 'Rokeby' is dedicated. Scott had two visits to Rokeby, the first in the summer of 1809 when he saw the area in its full glory, and the second in 1811. His friend Morritt provided him with general and historical details of the area and, after studying these, he returned to Rokeby in the Autumn of 1812 where, in his daily retreat - a cave overlooking the River Greta - he produced the 30,000 word long poem 'Rokeby' which was published on January 1st, 1813. This romance, centred on Teesdale and dealing with the five days following the Civil War Battle of Marston Moor in 1644, also describes in great detail and beauty the landscape, folklore and history of the area.

Wackford Squeers at Dotheboys Hall

The writer Charles Dickens also visited Teesdale for a few days. After arriving at Greta Bridge on 31st January, 1838, he stayed at the 'King's Head', Barnard Castle and the 'Unicorn Inn', Bowes, whilst collecting information for his proposed novel on the Yorkshire schools. The result was 'Nicholas Nickleby' which earned him £4,500. This story of the schoolmaster Squeers and his Dotheboys Hall School is thought to be based upon William Shaw and his Academy. This building can still be seen today at the western end of Bowes Village. Whilst staying at the 'King's Head' he also got the inspiration for another story. Nearby, just below the Market Cross, was the shop of Thomas Humphreys. Just inside the door was the famous clock built by his son William. Dickens made their acquaintance after calling to find the time of day by the clock destined to become the title of his story 'Master Humphrey's Clock'.

One of the more recent visitors to the area was TV star, Hercules the Bear, who came upon an unsuspecting fisherman on the banks of the River Tees, below High Force, and almost 'frightened him to death'. A more frequently observed TV personality in the dale is David Bellamy, the 'Botanic Man', who, in fact, lives not far away, near Hamsterley Forest.

To conclude, mention must be made of Hannah Hauxwell, who captured the hearts of millions in Yorkshire Television's 'Too Long a Winter' programme of January 1973. In response to this and the subsequent book, 'Hannah in Yorkshire', thousands of letters and gifts poured in to her small Low Birk Hatt Farm in Baldersdale. Today they still arrive, as do visitors and well-wishers, but apart from the excitement and attention, everyday life has changed little, and although she now has an electricity supply, water still has to be carried from a nearby stream. Over the last 8 years Hannah has become a national celebrity as she and her primitive existence have been repeatedly featured on television, radio and in newspapers. However, many dalesfolk believe that there is no need for her to live such a 'Spartan existence', and that because she is not typical of a 'dalesman', a completely false impression about life in the dales may result. This may well be true, but Hannah is a pleasant, forthright, knowledgeable, interesting and independent person, who, as a 'free spirit', follows the life-style of her choosing.

Teesdale has also been the home of judges, scientists, historians, and for one day a great war leader!

Sir John Hullock of Barnard Castle, born in 1767, became a prominent judge and is buried in the church. Sir Roderick Murchison was a famous geologist who lived at King Street, Barnard Castle. His expedition to the Nile led to the finding of Lake Victoria. William Hutchinson who lived in a still existing large house on Galgate produced his History of Durham in 1794. It was the first work of its kind and he can be called an historian rather than an antiquary if only because of its complete nature.

Winston Churchill is said to have had a conference in a siding at Barnard Castle Station in 1942.

To conclude mention must be made of the TV weather girl, Wincie Willis, who has a house near Winston.

Such are the many talents that have been and are still found in Teesdale.

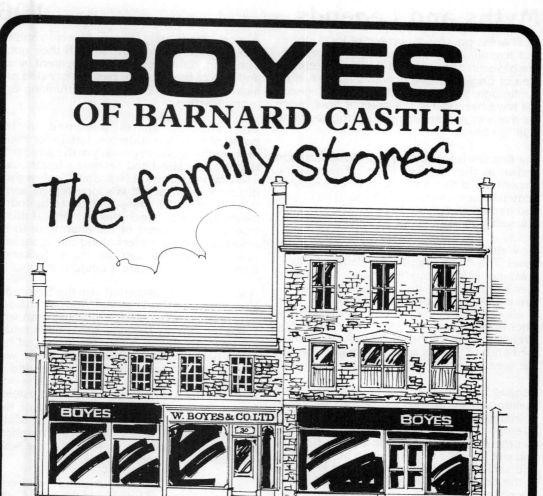

Myths and Legends

Most areas possess a number of local stories and legends, and Teesdale is no exception. We have already seen that this North Pennine area of England has a rich and varied history but though, sadly, many of the earlier legends will have been lost in the mists of time, there are many others remaining to stir the heart and chill the blood.

Our first tale is based upon the old superstition known as the 'Hand of Glory'. This was the ancient belief that if the hand of an executed criminal was severed from the hanging corpse and treated and pickled in a special way then it would possess certain powers.

Sir Walter Scott referred to this practice in his novel 'The Antiquary'. These 'Hands of Glory', grasping lighted candles made from dead men's fat, were reputed to have the power of striking all in their presence motionless - that is all except for the owners. Therefore the witches who used to prepare these hands had a ready market for their evil produce amongst the bands of thieves and robbers who roamed the area.

Legend has it that at the inn of Spital in the Stainmore Pass, in the October of 1797, such a 'Hand of Glory' was used in a robbery attempt. The inn keeper at this time was George Alderson and it was late on that cold and wet October evening when he, his family and servant girl Bella heard a loud knocking at the door. It was an old woman dressed in a long hooded cloak, and after offering her shelter and their hospitality, the family retired to bed leaving her with Bella in front of the fire.

However, Bella became suspicious and so pretended to fall asleep. Thinking she was asleep, the visitor removed the hooded cloak, revealing not a feeble old woman but a tall and powerful man. The stranger than placed a gruesome 'Hand of Glory' upon the table, fixed a candle in its grasp and having lit the candle called on the powers of the charm to ensure that those who were sleeping in the inn, remained asleep.

He then went outside to call in the rest of his band but Bella had been awake and she jumped up, locked and bolted the inn door, and rushed to arouse the family. But she could not awaken them and being greatly worried at hearing the villains banging on the inn door she remembered the lighted candle. Rushing downstairs she seized a cup of milk, doused the candle and broke the spell.

Almost immediately George Alderson and his son were at her side armed with their guns. The gang, disheartened at the apparent failure and loss of their charm, hastily retreated and all was saved by Bella's quick thinking and prompt action.

The withered charm remained in the possession of the Alderson family for many years until it was lost, possibly at the same time that the inn closed and became a farmhouse. The new inn is sited at New Spital, only a short distance away, and it is suggested by some that the 'Hand of Glory' is there to be found on the moors between the two inns. If this is true and the powers of the charm are to be believed, then travellers along this moorland road had best be watchful for its flickering flame and the dangers it could bring.

Another legend associated with the Stainmore Pass is that of the beautiful Norman maiden who was brutally beheaded by the man who loved her, simply because she did not return his love. To this very day the stories of her ghost haunting the routeway over these wild moors are still told. Her body is reputed to have been thrown into the well which is now found in the old cellars of a nearby hostelry. I have heard it said that the blood of this maiden is now found in the very walls of the building and that at certain times throughout history, her blood has flowed from the walls into this ancient well.

Stainmore Pass has a reputation for murders starting with that of Eric Bloodaxe in 954, and in fact the owner of this above mentioned hostelry, Mark Johns, was murdered a number of years ago. It seems that the tragedy of the Pass is not over.

Another ghost story is that of a duel between Sir John Musgrove and Stephen Bainbridge for the love of Edith Blakeney. Sir John Musgrove, who had travelled far and been associated with Raleigh and Drake, lived at Cleatlam Hall and was well liked in the district. But his love for Edith Blakeney had been forestalled by Stephen Bainbridge, 15 years his junior.

One night Musgrove found them together, just after a local 'wise' woman had claimed that there would be blood on his hands before he wedded Edith. Sir John challenged him to a duel at the Druid's Oak, where Cleatlam Lane met the main road. Sir John arrived home that night with his cloak spattered with blood. Stephen's horse arrived home without its rider. Stephen was found stabbed in the heart.

It was later agreed, however, that Bainbridge had fallen in fair combat. But there was to be no marriage. Edith Blakeney was never happy again and died within the year. Sir John departed from Cleatlam and may have died fighting the Turks. It is said that one autumn night, a knight on a white horse appears near Cleatlam, in ghostly white. It is reputed to be the lamenting ghost of Stephen Bainbridge.

Another legend involving love and a beautiful woman is that of 'The Singing Lady'. This tale began in the C19th at a small mineshop only a short distance to the west of the cascading falls of Cauldron Snout. At this time men were struggling hard to extract lead and barytes from the wild, remote Pennine Hills. The miners often lived great distances away and had to lodge in the mineshop throughout their working days - perhaps returning home to their wives and families only every fortnight. Our tale involves one of these miners and one of the women who were employed at the mineshop to wash, cook and perhaps serve drinks to the miners in the evening.

Our Singing Lady is the ghost of one of these women (I have called her Jenny not only because I feel that was her name but because it relates to the rare and beautiful wild flowers, the gentians, which are found nearby). She had been a young, innocent and beautiful country girl when she became friends with one of the miners. It is easy to imagine how they fell deeply in love and one can almost hear their laughter dancing over the fells. Sadly, however, the laughter turned to tears when one evening the miner told her their love affair was ended.

Later that night, in her grief and despair, she made her way towards the roar of Cauldron Snout and after pausing for an instant, threw herself into the foaming waters below. It is said that in the dark of night when the moon appears from behind the clouds and lights up the moors her beautiful figure can be seen shimmering ghostly white and sitting on the rock from which she made that fatal plunge into the cold water below.

Perhaps if you listen carefully through the sounds of the wind and the running waters, then you may well believe that you can hear her crying out or singing her sad love song. It is sad to think of her so alone and unhappy but it may be that she is waiting for her lover to return and then instead of her sad love song echoing through the night we may hear the sound of their laughter ringing over the fells once more.

The Singing Lady at Cauldron Snout

But tragic tales are not confined to love stories, they are also related to the livelihood of the area .In the higher reaches of Upper Teesdale, weather conditions in winter can be excessively severe. In the winter of 1836, John Allison and Bill Ritson, two shepherds, left the farm in Birkdale to save numerous sheep from certain death. Having pulled many sheep from the 'Wheel', a deep part of the River Tees , they started back to the farm. But conditions were so difficult that they could hardly make their way. John Allison stumbled and injured himself and Bill Ritson had to drag him for miles. When eventually they were found it was too late for 33 year old John Allison, although Bill Ritson survived. It was a high price to pay for his care of his sheep. The farm at Birkdale still stands and can still be cut off for months in winter as Brian Bainbridge, who farms there today, well knows.

The bleak, unpredictable hills have claimed quite a number of lives, including inexperienced tourists and fell walkers. Since 1947, which saw major snowstorms, there have been two excessively bad winters - that in 1962 and 1979. In fact 1979's winter in some ways equalled 1947 in severity and one life was lost in the dale that year because of it.

There are many other legends of the area including those of the three ghosts of Raby Castle. These include Charles Neville (the 6th Earl of Northumberland), Sir Henry Vane the Younger, and the 1st Lady Barnard, all of whom have their own particular reasons for wandering the castle that was once their home.

Sporting Activities

The Teesdale Area of the High Pennines offers quite a wide selection of physical activities for the sporting enthusiast. As a result it is really quite difficult to know where to start to describe them. Perhaps since this is an area of outstanding natural beauty we should first of all look at walking because this is not only a way of exercising but also an ideal way of enjoying the beautiful countryside.

In this guide we have selected four walks for more detailed description; however, if one was to look at an Ordnance Survey Map (scale 1:50,000 or 1:25,000) then it would become immediately apparent that the numerous public footpaths offer hundreds of possible routes for the walker.

We must stress, however, that before a person undertakes any walk he should be fully experienced and fully equipped.

For the long distance 'professional' walker there are many routes of interest but possibly none so popular as the well-known Pennine Way. This was the first long-distance footpath to be completed and is actually the second longest footpath in Britain and runs for 250 miles from the Peak District of Derbyshire northwards along the Pennines over the Cheviot Hills to the Scottish Border.

A very important part of this footpath runs through the Teesdale area of the High Pennines passing by the famous landforms of High Force and Cauldron Snout and passing over the summit of the 2930 ft (893 metres) Cross Fell. Youth Hostels are often used as resting places by walkers, and these can be found at (S to N) Dentdale, Hawes, Garsdale Head, Keld, KIRKBY STEPHEN, BALDERHEAD, BARNARD CASTLE, DUFTON, LANGDON BECK, ALSTON, Ninebanks (Allendale) and Once Brewed (near the Roman Wall).

Whilst on the topic of walking, Top Notch Sportswear of Market Place, Barnard Castle have raised a matter which demands much consideration!

If you run or walk just two miles a day, by the end of the year each foot will have hit the ground 650,000 times. What you wear on your feet to cushion and cope with that repeated impact can make the difference between jogging to fitness and running into some decidedly unhealthy foot, leg and back problems.

Every runner runs in a different way, but however you run, your foot comes under shock. If your shoe doesn't cushion the impact, the foot, parts of the leg and as far up as the hip and spine can be injured. Bone fractures, tendon problems, shin problems; these are all typical running injuries. Consequently, the better the shoe, the lower the risk of injury. These rules are true for any sport you may wish to participate in. With very few exceptions, you get what you pay for with footwear.

Therefore, if you need footwear or clothing covering a wide range of sporting activities, why not call in at Top Notch Sportswear for an excellent choice and perhaps some welcome help and advice.

The landscape of the area also provides for highly specialised sports such as rock climbing and underground exploration. With official permission groups of organised 'potholers' explore not only this limestone area but also the old lead and barytes mines. However, once again we give you warning - this time against entering any such features because weathering and decay, for example, could result in a fatal fall of rock.

The geology of the area provides an ideal training ground for mountaineers and rock-climbers. However, permission must first be obtained from the landowners before you venture on to their property. Holwick Scars at Holwick near Middleton-in-Teesdale have been a popular spot for rock-climbers for quite a long time now. Unfortunately the privilege of climbing on the 'Scars' is not welcomed by the farmer concerned and has been suspended by the owner of the Strathmore Estate.

For the non-walkers who still wish to exercise whilst enjoying the country air and the beautiful landscape, riding and pony trekking facilities are available. There is some marvellous riding country in Teesdale and extensive bridleways enable one to make full use of this feature. What better way of admiring the moorland scenery than from the back of a horse? Anyone interested in riding holidays or day rides should contact Mrs. Killen at West Park in Lunedale.

We know that Teesdale is located amongst some of the highest peaks in England, so it may be a surprise to note the variety of water-based sports that are to be found. These include sailing, water-skiing, fine boat rowing, windsurfing and, of course, angling which is very popular. All these activities are provided by the Northumbrian Water Authority (N.W.A.) who control most of the 'waters' in the area covered by this guide.

Sailing takes place at Selset Reservoir through membership of the Selset Sailing Club which is based on its northern shore, waterskiing takes place at Balderhead Reservoir through membership of the Balderhead Water Ski Club and fine-boat rowing is available at Hury Reservoir through membership of the Selset Oarsmen Club.

However, perhaps the most rapidly flourishing sport is that of canoeing, and on the fine white-water stretches of the River Tees, a growing number of canoeists and many events are to be seen throughout the year. These include British Canoe Union Ranking Events, both in the Slalom discipline and White Water Racing.

Nevertheless, angling continues to be the best supported of all the activities, but please remember that any person fishing in the N.W.A. area must first of all obtain a rod licence and secondly a day, week or season permit for the locality in which they are to fish. The N.W.A. reservoirs offer seasonal worm and fly fishing - the Hury, Blackton, Balderhead and Cow Green reservoirs are stocked only with the native brown trout, whereas the Selset and Grassholme reservoirs also stock rainbow trout. However, although some fishermen would rather accept the challenge of the fast flowing rivers, it must be remembered that many riverbanks are privately owned. Permits are available for certain stretches such as parts of the north and south banks of the River Tees west of Middleton-in-Teesdale. Details about permits can be sought at the local tourist information centres.

Other sports of the area include the traditional game shooting on the grouse moors but now there is also clay pigeon and target shooting provided by the Teesdale Gun Club and the Teesdale Pistol and Rifle Club respectively. Details of membership and the possibility of tuition and practice may be obtained from The Gun Shop at Barnard Castle.

During the last decade, Teesdale has been becoming increasingly popular as a venue for outdoor sports and adventure activities, many of which have been described above. Its natural resources spread over many miles have attracted people from the distant parts of Britain, but it has been with the development of professional outdoor activity centres such as the Pace Outdoor Centre at Forest-in-Teesdale, and Hudeway in Middleton-in-Teesdale, that an organised and educational approach has been achieved.

The establishments have created the staffed residential facility essential to attract specialist groups and extended families to the dale for sport, training and recreation. Indeed, the National Youth Slalom team underwent squad training whilst staying at Hudeway.

In addition, Adventure Activity Holidays for the Young which have been long established in the south and west, are proving very popular in Teesdale. At Hudeway, Alan Graham, a lecturer in Outdoor Education at a teacher training college and resident of the dale, has pioneered, together with his wife and seasonal staff, multi-activity holidays for unaccompanied children.

For further details about courses and lessons in a variety of activities including windsurfing, contact Alan Graham at Hudeway.

The other activity centre found in the dale is that of the Pace Outdoor Centre which is highly organised and has an excellent and growing reputation. Located some eight miles west of Middleton-in-Teesdale, it possesses a picturesque rural setting and ideal base from where the Centre's own transport can take advantage of the varied natural and man-made features and facilities throughout the area.

This residential centre offers a wide variety of activities from guided walks to rock climbing, and sailing lessons in dinghies should also be available in the near future.

If you are looking for a family day out with a distinctive regional flavour, there are plenty of agricultural shows and other country activities such as sheepdog trials, native pony breed shows, country fairs and driving trials, all of which are held at frequent intervals during the summer months. These are well advertised locally and are usually an easy drive away from Teesdale.

To conclude, mention must be made of the 18-hole golf courses at Barnard Castle and Appleby, the 9-hole golf course at Alston, the tennis and bowls facilities at Bowes Museum, and, of course, for the winter sports specialist the winter ski-slopes of Upper Teesdale. Another alternative for a rainy day is a game of squash at The Grand Prix Club, Brough, or at Lartington Hall near Barnard Castle.

Whatever your interests, you should find plenty to keep you busy during your visit to Teesdale. Enjoy our beautiful dale!

The Old Manor House Hotel

The Old Manor House in West Auckland is a picturesque building steeped in history and so full of atmosphere and charm that it hardly seems like an Hotel at all ... Parts of the building date back to the 13th Century and the owners have retained its essential olde worlde character with a rich blend of antique and reproduction furnishings.

The proprietors of this remarkable hotel, the Cleminson family, pride themselves on giving their guests such a good personal service that the Manor House becomes more like a visit to friends.

Seventeenth century buildings annexed to the Manor House provide more bedrooms, banqueting facilities and an exciting range of recreational amenities including an Indoor heated swimming pool (the first in this area) Sauna, jaccuzi and Solarium. The whole complex is tastefully designed and furnished to a high standard.

One of the foremost attractions of The Old Manor House Hotel is its high standard of cuisine, complemented with a well stocked wine cellar. The quality of food from an extensive menu has earned the Jacobean Restaurant a well deserved reputation.

Many companies use the Old Manor House as a Conference Centre and Exhibition venue. The Hotel offers a business-like yet relaxed atmosphere with efficient staff to help the occasion become successful. Repeat bookings for meetings and conferences of numbers between 12 and 150 prove the Hotel's popularity.

The "Knights Hall" banqueting hall seats 150 people for medieval banquets in the Olde Worlde Baronial splendour with large log fire, suits of armour and beamed ceiling.

Most of the hotels 30 bedrooms have been left in character of yesteryear but all include modern day conveniences. Full en-suite facilities, direct dial Telephone, Colour T.V., Radio, Trouser Press, Hairdryer, plus Tea and Coffee making facilities are supplied in all rooms.

The Knights Hall is used quite often for wedding celebrations and one of the special services offered to the bride and groom is use of the Hotel's Rolls Royce Car to transport them in style to the Church and then to the Hotel for the Reception afterwards. Functions Catered for.

WEST AUCKLAND, CO. DURHAM
Telephone: (0388) 832504 & 832358

West Auckland is a small village yet boasts the largest Village Green in the Country. It is situated very close to Darlington and Bishop Auckland with easy access to main line trains, the A1(M) Motorway and Teesside Airport.

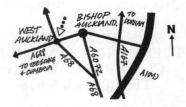

Crafts and Craftsmen

Over the centuries man has had to fashion and shape his own tools, clothing and equipment entirely by hand. Some of these skills included the manufacture of items from wood and metals, the weaving of cloth and the making of clothes, rugs, quilts, baskets and pottery. Examples of other past crafts are those of butter and cheese making which were practised on many farms in the area with the produce being sold at the local market and possibly also at the Buttermarket (now the Market Cross) in Barnard Castle.

The skills that were acquired by craftsmen were passed down from generation to generation but today the numbers of craftsmen have sadly declined. This is a direct result of the mass-production techniques arising from increased technology following the Industrial Revolution of the C18th. It is fortunate that these skills have not completely died out and that many are still practised in Teesdale today, though possibly in most cases now merely as a hobby. However, not only are some old crafts still essential today, such as those of the dry-stone waller and the blacksmith, but also some crafts are kept alive by dedicated individual craftsmen who strive to earn a living from their inborn skills.

Heighington Forge is the Blacksmiths Shop of Stephen Jackson. Located beside the A68 on the outskirts of the village of Heighington, Stephen established his craft workshop here in February 1984 and has continued to expand despite the major setbacks of a fire in his premises in June 1985. Among the items that are produced here are ornamental ironwork, made-to-measure garden gates, garden furniture, iron railings and fire baskets. If you have 'something special' that you require, then why not enquire as to whether Stephen can be of assistance. Maintaining the links with farming, Heighington Forge also repairs farm equipment and supplies all types of agricultural iron.

Craftsman Alistair Brookes has enjoyed a growing reputation throughout the north for his 'pottery figures' since opening his Mickleton Pottery in 1975. Mickleton is a small working village of stone-built houses sited next to the River Tees 8 miles (13kms) west of Barnard Castle and 2 miles (3kms) east of Middleton-in-Teesdale. Here he produces pottery figures modelled on local people, past and present, who have made or make their living farming, quarrying and mining in this rugged part of the Pennine Hills. All his products are individually made as he successfully resists the temptation to expand into large-scale commercial production, thus preserving his individuality. Some recent additions to his range are coal-mining figures and typical Teesdale farmhouses and barns. As well as having his characteristic figures and buildings, his showroom, which being open to the public, is an obvious tourist attraction, also has the characteristic range of domestic earthenware and stoneware.

Peter and Sonia Kempsey are the owners of the Gossipgate Galleries in Alston, found near a secluded spot near the Gossipgate Packhorse Bridge and Stepping Stones. The range of art and craft work is extensive and is derived from Cumbria, Durham and Northumberland. Peter and Sonia converted the building, which was formerly a Congregational chapel. The Gallery is also their home where they live and work, and welcome visitors. As well as the art and craft work, the Alston Historical Society have a small exhibition of local history, and the chapel's original gaslights have been re-connected to provide the necessary atmosphere. The main exhibits are not necessarily historical, however, but are today's craftmanship, and there is often a special exhibition centred on the work of one person or a group. The Galleries are open seven days a week from spring to Christmas and today, when there are few places displaying the contemporary work of local artists, it is refreshing to find this gallery in our area. All the exhibits are displayed with the purpose of being sold.

At the Art Cellar in Kirkby Stephen there are paintings and craft work, but also pottery and knitwear, jewellery, prints and cards making it an 'Aladdin's Cave' of art with prices to suit your pocket. For the craftsman, it is not only important to make beautiful objects, but that he receives some return for all the work he has put in.

Roy and Margaret Thomas, local art enthusiasts from Middleton, have developed the mobile 'Teesdale Galleries'. These are held usually at Bank Holidays at various venues in the area, when large numbers of paintings by local and national artists are displayed with a wide price range.

We may ask what is the definition of a craftsman? One who does skilled handiwork in whatever medium he may choose? But does this exclude work on machines ..... and obviously there is even some overlap with engineers and scientists. Nevertheless, the nature and character of the dales Craftsmen is clearly evident.

ALDBROUGH ST.JOHN A small village beside the B6275 Roman road known as Dere Street. Sited beside the Aldbrough Beck 3 miles S of Piercebridge.

ALSTON (described elsewhere)

ARMATHWAITE Attractive village. Possesses C14th pele tower and was the site of a Benedictine nunnery. The nuns were poor compared to many Cumbrian medieval religious houses, and the area was subject to frequent Scottish raids. The castle belonged to the Skelton family until 1712, and the young Edward II is said to have stayed there, before he became king. Its station lay on the Midland railway's route to Scotland but is now closed.

BARNARD CASTLE (Described in detail elsewhere)

BARNINGHAM A small village 2 miles S of Greta Bridge. The Church of St. Michael, built in 1816 and altered in 1891, replaces an earlier Norman church. On Barningham Moor many prehistoric finds have been discovered.

BOLAM A small rural village on the northern edge of the Tees valley 2 miles NE of Ingleton. Said to have been originally a larger medieval village, now much shrunken. Original site known as Old Bolam.

BOLDRON A small village 2 miles SW of Barnard Castle. Like Bowes and Richmond, considerable parts of this village were owned in the Middle Ages by the dukes of Britanny of Richmond Castle. Just off two Roman roads, but still a quiet backwater.

BOWBANK Small sheltered hamlet on B6276 through Lunedale, and not far south of Middleton-in-Teesdale. Once had a coaching inn on the road to Brough.

BOWES (Described elsewhere)

BOWLEES Hamlet on the B6277 beside the Bowlees Beck to the north of the River Tees. Name means 'clearing with the curving boundary'. Its former Primitive Methodist Chapel, built in 1868, is now the Bowlees Visitors Centre. The Summerhill Force Waterfall and Gibson's Cave are only a short distance away.

BRIGNALL A small village 1 mile SW of Greta Bridge and N of the River Greta. The manor was once held by the Earl of Britanny and later the Scropes. An important family there, the Philips, were involved in a strange tale of witchcraft in which their family was cursed.

At any rate the family died without issue by 1575. There are remains of the water mill with an internal undershot wheel. Sir Walter Scott celebrated the banks of Brignall in his poem 'Rokeby' and the old church of St. Mary is the subject of a drawing by the famous artist Turner. The ruins of the C13th church can still be seen although it was partly demolished. A new church was then built at the top of the bank (consecrated 1835, restored 1892). The Brignall Banks 'so mild and fair' are a popular spot for walkers.

BROUGH (Described in detail elsewhere)

CALDWELL A small village beside the Caldwell Beck 3 miles SE of Winston on the open rolling farmland of the broad lower dale.

COTHERSTONE An attractive village to the S of the River Tees about 3 miles NW of Barnard Castle. Has a Quaker Meeting House built in 1797 with its own graveyard. The Church of St. Cuthbert has a fine spire (almost the only one in Teesdale) although it replaced an earlier one. The dedication to St. Cuthbert was given on the assumption that the village was Cuthbertstun, a village mentioned in a document of 1050, but this has since proved to be untenable. It is Cathere's settlement as it appears in Domesday Book of 1086 when the village is said to be waste. The Fitzhughs who held the manor of the Earls of Richmond (Dukes of Britanny) in the Middle Ages, built their castle on the Hagg. It is described as a fortified house in 1201 but was probably further developed later. It may have been burned down in the Scots raids at the beginning of the C14th, and today there is little trace of it.

There are a number of fine Georgian houses towards the east end of the village around the green. Interesting farms in the vicinity include Doe Park, a largely C18th mansion house, providing memories of a deer park there. Wodencroft was once a school where Richard Cobden, the leading radical, and founder of the Anti-Corn Law League, attended. Here, near the confluence of the Rivers Balder and Tees, a mound is said to have been a Norse temple and certainly the name Balder celebrates a Scandinavian god.

DALTON A small village beside the Dalton Beck 6 miles SE of Barnard Castle. Just to the south is the almost 2000 year old Brigantian fort known as Castle Steads.

DIRT PIT A hamlet in the valley known as

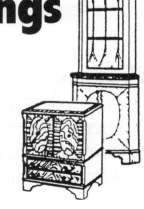

Ettersgill about 4 miles NW of Middleton-in-Teesdale. The name probably means just what it says, or it may be as is often suggested, 'deer path', linking it with the ancient forest of Teesdale. The monks of Rievaulx Abbey, who had lodges at Friar House (originally Frere House - the Norman French for Brother) and at Hope House near Middleton, are said to have built a chapel at Dirt Pit which may have survived the Reformation in the C16th.

EAST LAYTON A small village with a church, ancient hall and moat about 1 mile N of A66(T) and 6 miles SE of Greta Bridge.

EGGLESTON A small village located to the N of the River Tees between Barnard Castle and Middleton-in-Teesdale. First mentioned in 1196 as 'Egleston' meaning Ecgwulf's homestead. An ancient stone circle was sadly removed to repair roads! Once a major lead smelting centre in the C19th but no trace remains today. Eggleston Hall owned by Lady Gray is a fine building, now used as a Finishing School for Girls. The Kielder Tunnel from Weardale enters the Tees a short distance below the old Eggleston Bridge.

EPPELBY A small rural village beside the Aldbrough Beck 4 miles SE of Winston.

FORCETT A hamlet on the B6274, 4 miles SE of Winston. Has a church and is near to Forcett Hall and Park. To the east is the 1900 years old Brigantian earthwork defences known as the Stanwick Fortifications.

FOREST-IN-TEESDALE Called a village sometimes but it is really an area of widely dispersed farmsteads between High Force and Langdon Beck. The ancient forest of Teesdale was so called because it was a hunting area for the Baliols and later Lords. An iron-age maiden is said to have been discovered in the Teesdale caves along with Roman coins. Usually the forest is spoken of North of the Tees, but in documents the south side is also known as the Forest. Has a post office, chapel (once 3) and the Church of St.James The Less.

GAINFORD A large village with an attractive village green beside the A67 on the N bank of the River Tees. The oldest part of the village was designated as a conservation area in 1971. The major attraction is the Jacobean Mansion finished in 1605 for the local vicar, John Cradock. Within the grounds of this Gainford Hall can be seen a C17th Elizabethan dovecote. About half a mile upstream is the sulphurous spring, known as Gainford Spa, which led to the development of some

boarding houses for visitors. However it is a very old settlement once being called Geganford, meaning 'direct ford'. The old St. Mary's Church which dates from about 1200 is built on the site of an even earlier church, possibly the Genforda Monastery where the Northumbrian Chief Ida or Eda was buried in 801. A 'Walkabout' leaflet has been produced by the County Planning Department for this village with so much to offer, and, according to a local saying, "where the Parson married a Pigg, christened a Lamb and buried a Hogg". It has even been suggested that the old foundations discovered in a field near to the Hall were those of an ancient castle. The castle may have been constructed by Bishop Bek, who is known to have done building work here. Before this date Agnes de Valenum, the widow of one of the Baliol family, had gallows here, and in the late Anglo-Saxon period Gainford was the head village of a great estate.

GARRIGILL A small peaceful village beside the youthful River South Tyne and near to the B6277 road from Teesdale to Alston. The 'Straits of Garrigill' is an interesting river feature in the village. Nearby is the impressive Ashgill Force. On the old miners' route from the Pennine Fells to Alston and on the track over the Pennines from Dufton to Alston.

GAYLES A hamlet with an old hall about 8 miles SE of Barnard Castle. About 1000 metres to the west is the 2000 year-old circular hill fort known as Castle Steads. It is believed to have been built by the Brigantes as they prepared to meet the Roman advance some 1900 years ago.

GILMONBY A historic hamlet on the south bank of the River Greta opposite the village of Bowes. It is reputed that during the C13th the village was given to the Norman Sheriff, Ranulph de Glanville, by the Abbot Savericus. This was conditional on an inn and facilities being maintained to serve the Abbot and his attendants. The old Gilmonby Hall is said to have at one time incorporated the village green into its gardens.

GRAINS O' TH' BECK A bleak, remote hamlet on the B6276 from Middleton-in-Teesdale to Brough via Lunedale. The 'grains' are the Arngill and Lunehead Becks that unite to form the River Lune. The Old Norse word 'greinn' also means branch - the becks being the branches of the River Lune. Sited at the bridging point of these becks a few metres above their confluence. In the coaching days

an inn was to be found here. This was also once the site of a popular livestock show.

GRETA BRIDGE A hamlet 3 miles SE of Barnard Castle near the attractive bridge with stone balustrades that crosses the River Greta and which was built by J.B.S. Morritt of the nearby Rokeby Hall in 1789. Today the village is by-passed by the A66(T). a Roman camp was found not far from the bridge. It was at the 'New Inn', now Thorpe Grange, that Charles Dickens stayed on 31/1/1838.

HARWOOD A dispersed settlement of farmsteads occupying the valley of the Harwood Beck and stretching for about 4 miles W of the hamlet of Langdon Beck. A methodist chapel stands alone in the centre of the valley. In the past many of the farmers were also miners at the Lady Rake Lead Mine.

HEADLAM A hamlet with a magnificent old hall located just over 1 mile N of Gainford on rolling farmland of the lower dale.

HILTON A small rural village with an old hall. Sited on the gently rolling farmland about 3 miles ENE of Staindrop.

HOLWICK A dispersed settlement to the S of the river in Upper Teesdale. Once the most northerly village in Yorkshire, but now in County Durham. Located below the lofty, dark, whinstone cliffs of Holwick Scar and Castles. An old settlement on the ancient 'green road' over the Pennines via Cronkley Scar and the Maize Beck. Nearby is the Fairy Dell waterfall as well as the haunted Park End Wood, a remnant of the original Forest of Teesdale. Holwick Hall, now owned by the Earl of Strathmore (the nephew of the Queen Mother) was built for Cosmo Bonsor MP in the late C19th. It was on Holwick Fell on April 8th, 1794 that Shepherd William Robinson of Hungry Hall Farm, was murdered.

HUNDERTHWAITE A hamlet of Scandinavian origin just to the SW of Romaldkirk. One suggestion is that the name is derived from 'Hunrothr's thwaite' meaning 'Hunrothr's clearing'. Another belief is that its name resulted from the word 'Hundredskelde' meaning 'the one hundred springs'. In 1070 King Malcolm of Scotland raided the area and met the men of Teesdale in battle at Hunderthwaite. Sadly most of the dalesmen were killed and the area laid waste.

HUTTON MAGNA A small village with a church, hall, and unusual inn 2 miles SE of Whorlton.

In a rural setting beside the Hutton Beck. The church of St. Mary the Virgin was rebuilt in 1889 on the site of earlier churches.

INGLETON A small ribbon village on the B6279 3 miles E of Staindrop. Has a Methodist Chapel and the Church of St. John (built in 1843). The first mention of this settlement was in 1050 when it was Ingletun (Ingeld's farm or village).

KILLERBY A small village on the Killerby Beck just N of the B6279 4 miles E of Staindrop. First mentioned as Culuerdebi (Kilvert's village) in 1091.

KINNINVIE A hamlet located on the B6279 4 miles W of Staindrop overlooking Langleydale. Has an old Methodist Chapel and one of the smallest inns in the dale.

KIRKBY HILL A small, rural settlement about 8 miles SE of Barnard Castle and 1 mile S of Ravensworth. Much of interest in the vicinity, such as Ravensworth Castle, Castle Steads and the historic town of Richmond with its fine castle (some 4 miles to the SE).

LAITHKIRK A hamlet beside the River Lune about 1 mile S of Middleton-in-Teesdale. Its little church, dating from the mid C15th and restored in 1898, served Mickelton, Lunedale and Holwick. The building was once the tithe barn of Lord Fitzhugh. There was once an inn here in the coaching days of old. An inscription on its wall stated "Good Ale, Pipes and Tobacco: If by you go And dry you be, The fault's in you And not in me".

LANGDON BECK A hamlet in Upper Teesdale beside the beck of the same name. Once the site of an old lead smelting mill and lead mine. The Langdon Beck Hotel/Inn was built in 1887 to replace the Sportsman's Rest, or Traveller's Rest as it was also known, on the opposite side of the road.

LANGTON A small village beside the Langton Beck on the rolling farmland of the lower dale about 2 miles N of Gainford. First referred to as Langadun (long hill) about 1050.

LANGWATHBY Village with magnificent village green. The Church of St.Peter was built in 1718. In the Middle Ages there was just a Chantry Chapel here but some of the old chapel survives, particularly the north arcade of three bays.

LARTINGTON A small village to the S of the

The Brown Jug Inn

Residential Free House

You will find a warm friendly atmosphere at this charming Inn, which offers an extensive range of Bar Meals, available every lunch time and evening, throughout the week. Come and see our unique collection of jugs and our friendly spiders. We can also offer first class accommodation; our rooms having central heating and en-suite bathrooms. Large Car Park, Children's Play Area, Beer Garden, Sitting on the side of the A688 twixt West Auckland and Raby Castle.

Evenwood Gate, Nr. West Auckland, Co. Durham DL14 9NW. Tel: (0388) 833180

DRIVE INN MOTEL

Telephone for Free Brochure

Telephone (0388) 663885

- ● 40 Bedrooms with bath & shower, colour television and telephone.
- ● Special all inclusive weekend rates.
- ● 'TRAX' over 25 Discotheque, all Hotel residents gain free admission to this exclusive club for the duration of their stay.
- ● Full conference and function facilities for up to 200 persons.
- ● A new motel ideally situated for historical sightseeing in Northumberland, Durham and The North Riding of Yorkshire.

- ● "Bugatti' Restaurant with Sophisticated a la carte menu.
- ● Carvery featured and table d'hote menu is available.
- ● Lounge Bar
- ● "Stripes" Coffee Shop, modern decor with American style menu.

St. Helens Auckland, Bishop Auckland, Co. Durham On the A688 between Bishop Auckland and West Auckland.

River Tees 2 miles W of Barnard Castle. Once a single homestead. The present hall was built at the time of King Charles 1, but a hall has been in existence here for about 1000 years. In fact it was mentioned in the Domesday Book of 1086. The present hall, which had a private chapel and museum is now privately owned. Lartington Park has been the location of The Teesdale Country Fair which was conceived in 1975.

LAZONBY Village with Viking name like so many villages in Cumbria which came from Norse settlers in the C10th from Ireland who met with few Saxon settlers already here.

Lazonby boasts a station, not used by regular traffic but Dales excursion trains, and a fine open-air swimming pool.

The manor was owned by King John, but Henry gave it, along with some others, to the Scots in compensation for loss of the Northern counties. However, with the defection of John Baliol in 1294, Edward I took it back. It was later granted to Ralph Neville of Raby, then came to Richard, Duke of Gloucester. Finally it descended to the Duke of Devonshire.

The Roman Fort - Old Penrith, is at Plumpton.

The manor was owned by the Stutevilles, Morvilles, Multons, Dacres, and Musgraves in succession.

There is a Victorian Church of 1863. The original church of Lazonby was given to Lanercost Priory. There were said formerly to have been Roman monuments in the churchyard.

LITTLE NEWSHAM A small village with a church, one mile NW of Winston. Once on the now-dismantled Darlington - Barnard Castle railway.

LONTON A hamlet located on the road between Mickleton and Middleton-in-Teesdale, to the S of the River Tees.

MELMERBY Village 9 miles NE by E of Alston, 10 miles SW of Penrith. Attractive village green and a Victorian church. Melmerby Hall's main buildings are Georgian, but the wings are of the C17th. The village used to be famous for its mid-summer bonfire - a survival of fire worship, but it was replaced by cattle fairs in the last century. For a time a college of eight Chantry priests was founded in the Church in 1387. Two natural features are of note - here the Helm wind can be felt

in all its violence and above the village is the Melmerby Scar famous for its limestone of a particularly light coloured type free from impurities.

MICKLETON A ribbon village over a mile long on the S bank of the River Tees. Originated as a single enclosure amidst the widespread woodland. The name means 'large farm'. 500 metres to the south is Bail Green, where in 1832 an early bronze-age burial mound revealed a corpse. Its crouched position with knees up to the chin is a characteristic of the 'Beaker Folk'. The village green was lost as a result of enclosure.

MIDDLETON-IN-TEESDALE (Described in detail elsewhere)

NEWBIGGIN A village 2 miles NW of Middleton-in-Teesdale beside the B6277 to the N of the River Tees. First mentioned about 1316 as 'Neubiggin' meaning 'new building'. Farming and mining settlement with the Redgroves and Pikelaw mines on the fells above and a smelting mill in the village. Wesleyan Chapel built in 1760 and enlarged in 1860. Once a self-sufficient community with many shops and trades to be found.

NEWSHAM A small village 3 miles SE of Greta Bridge. In 1828 a village cross was erected and near to its base was fixed a set of iron stocks. These were last used in 1860 when a drunken shoemaker was punished for brawling in the village during a period of worship.

NORTH STAINMORE A small, dispersed settlement located in Stainmore Gap or Pass about 3 miles E of Brough. A rural area through which passes the A66(T) trans-Pennine route. This natural routeway, once followed by the Stainmore Glacier in the Ice Age, has been subject to the movements of man for over 5000 years. As a result it is not surprising to see the large number of historic remains along its length.

OUSBY Village 12½ miles SW of Alston. With characteristic Viking element in the name -by, the name is also said to come from Ulf or Olave, the son of Halfden, the Northern Viking leader. The church is a modern structure, but there is an early C14th effigy of a crusader in its chancel, and an ancient sedelin (seat) and piscina (basin for washing communion plate). Hall Farm is an C18th house in Classical style of 1743.

OVINGTON This small village S of the River Tees and 2 miles S of Winston was once known as the 'Maypole Village'. One famous pole was erected during the Diamond Jubilee of 1897, but the original maypole was "stolen" from Hutton Magna in the dead of night. To the west is the ancient, 2 hectare earthwork known as Cockshott Camp. The village is famous for its 'Four Alls Inn': the four alls being The Queen: "I govern all". A Soldier: "I fight for all". A Parson: "I pray for all". A Farmer: "I pay for all". Rather appropriate when one considers that this is a farming area.

PIERCEBRIDGE An attractive village located at the intersection of the A67 and the B6275 Roman road on the N bank of the River Tees. First mentioned about 1050 as 'Persebrigc' which means 'a light bridge'. The village is built on the site of a square Roman Camp built about 270 AD to protect the northbound Roman road known as Watling Street. The original bridge initiated by the Romans was virtually washed away without a trace in the floods of 1771. The present 3 arch bridge, which was built further upstream in 1600s severely damaged in the same floods and not fully repaired until 1797. St. Mary's Church was built in 1873. The old "George Inn" possessed the clock which provided the inspiration for the famous song 'My Grandfather's Clock'.

RAVENSWORTH A small village located SE of Greta Bridge. Tradition has that its C12th castle was built upon earlier Saxon defences. Belonging to the Fitzhugh family, it was visited by King John in 1202, but was largely demolished in the early C16th.

ROMALDKIRK Located to the S of the River Tees about 5 miles NW of Barnard Castle. The village is one of the most attractive in the area. The cruciform church of St. Romald dates from the C12th but was built on the site of an earlier Saxon church. The village was devastated by King Malcolm of Scotland in 1070. In 1644 the Plague claimed many lives. In the C17th there was a brewery in the village.

SCARGILL A hamlet 3 miles SW of Greta Bridge. Probably an old Norse settlement since 'gill' is the Norse word for ravine. Here can be seen the ruins of an old Pele Tower where the Lord of Scargill reputedly entertained King Edward in 1323. Foundations nearby are said by tradition to be the ruins of an old church. Ancient Roman shrines can be found on Scargill Moor.

SOUTH STAINMORE A picturesque, rural area of dispersed farmsteads lying between, and along the banks of the Augill Beck, Argill Beck and River Belah. On the southern slopes of the Stainmore Pass just beyond the border of the Yorkshire Dales National Park. One particularly fine building to be seen is the privately owned, attractive Augill Castle, built in 1842.

STAINDROP A large village with wide greens. First mentioned about 1050 as Standropa meaning stony place. Granted a charter for a weekly market and annual fair in 1378. This was retained until 1796 when Barnard Castle became the Market Town for the area. The Church of St. Mary is one of the most interesting in the area. Though added to over the centuries, this was originally a Saxon Church, the present building dating from the C12th. It is the burial place of the Neville Family who, for so long, held the nearby Raby Castle.

STAINTON A small village N of the A688 2 miles NE of Barnard Castle. Its famous sandstone quarries have provided much building stone. It was once reported that this stone was "the second choice of the House of Parliament".

STARTFORTH Once in Yorkshire at the southern end of the County Bridge over the Tees from Barnard Castle. At the meeting of the Roman road between the Roman forts of Lavatrae (Bowes) and Vinovium (Binchester, Bishop Auckland) and the ford across the River Tees therefore known as 'Streetford'. The present church was built in 1863 to replace an earlier C13th building. However, a C9th Saxon cross found here is an indication of an even earlier church, perhaps that mentioned in the Domesday Book (1086) as being sited at 'Stratford'. A famous landmark, Ullathorne Mill, was demolished in 1976, despite protest. This had been both a shoe-lace and rope-making mill.

THRINGARTH An old small hamlet on the B6276 2 miles SW of Middleton-in-Teesdale in Lunedale. The small chapel can still be seen.

WACKERFIELD A small settlement just S of the A688 3 miles NE of Staindrop. A Roman road passed the outskirts of the hamlet. The first record of the settlement was about 1050 when it was known as Wacarfield - an old English word meaning 'willow field'.

WEST AUCKLAND Village on Roman road to Binchester. Already in existence in 1050 AD. Said to have been a borough in one document, although this may be a mistake for

The River Tees below mighty Bernard's Castle(MP)

Bishop Auckland. Credited by some as having the longest village green in the country. The Eden family, so important here, can be traced back at least to Robert de Eden (born in the reign of Edward III and died in 1413.) They owned the Manor House at West Auckland which is on C12th foundations but is mainly C17th. A tower at the back of the building is certainly older. Two other fine C17th houses can be seen on the green, East Ockley House and The Old Hall.The most important historical event to the inhabitants must be that commemorated by the Sir Thomas Lipton Trophy in the Working Men's Club when West Auckland, with a team composed mainly of miners, won the world cup in 1910, and retained it in 1911.

WEST LAYTON A hamlet just N of the A66(T) 4 miles SE of Greta Bridge on the rolling farmland of the lower dale.

WHORLTON A small village 4 miles E of Barnard Castle on the N bank of the River Tees. Its church of St.Mary was rebuilt in 1853. Settlement first mentioned about 1050 as 'Queornington' meaning 'mill(stream)farm'. The present 53 metre-span suspension bridge

over the River Tees was commenced in 1830 after the foundations of a planned stone bridge had been washed away in 1829. Once a very dangerous ford on its site. The S bank of the river now has a very popular Lido and Picnic Area.

WINSTON A small village 6 miles E of Barnard Castle, beside the A67 on the N bank of the River Tees. First mentioned about 1091 as 'Winestona' which means 'Wine's farm'. The Church of St.Andrew was founded in 1254 but may have replaced an earlier church since some Saxon remains have been found. The Manor once belonged to the powerful Nevilles. Westholm Manor is a Jacobean building dating from 1606. The 33 metre, single-span, stone bridge built in 1765 for the carriage of coal, was thought to have been the largest in Europe at that time. It was one of the few bridges not washed away in the great floods of 1771.

WYCLIFFE A hamlet on the S bank of the River Tees 4 miles E of Barnard Castle. Traditionally believed to be the birthplace of the great church reformer John Wycliffe (1324). The tiny church of St.Mary the Virgin was rebuilt in the C13th on C8th foundations.

Index 126

Advertisers' Index